On the Coast

On the Coast

Mississippi Tales and Recipes

Troy Gilbert and Matthew Mayfield   Art by Billy Solitario

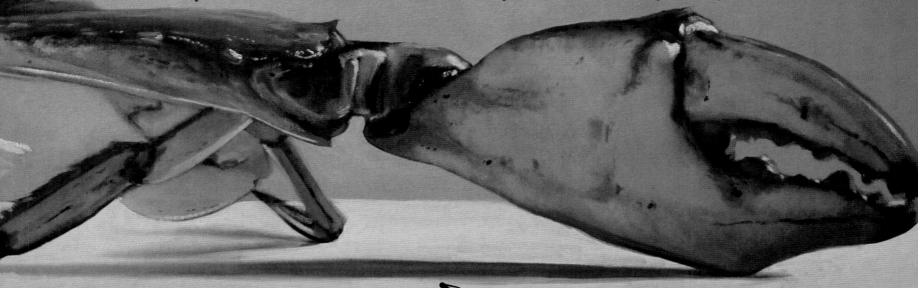

PELICAN PUBLISHING COMPANY

GRETNA 2017

*The word "Pelican" and the depiction of a pelican are
trademarks of Pelican Publishing Company, Inc., and are
registered in the U.S. Patent and Trademark Office.*

ISBN 9781455622559
E-book ISBN 9781455622566

*All photographs by Troy Gilbert unless otherwise noted. Photographs on pages 1, 5, 39, 51, 65,
73, 109, 164, 165, and 174 by Chris Granger.*

Printed in Malaysia

Published by Pelican Publishing Company, Inc.
1000 Burmaster Street, Gretna, Louisiana 70053

For the people of the Mississippi Gulf Coast,
who have endured everything
yet have never found a reason to stop laughing
or cooking or fishing

To understand the world, you must first
understand a place like Mississippi.
—William Faulkner

I like to eat crawfish and drink beer. That's despair?
—Walker Percy

We'll be dancing when we go.
—Jimmy Buffett

Contents

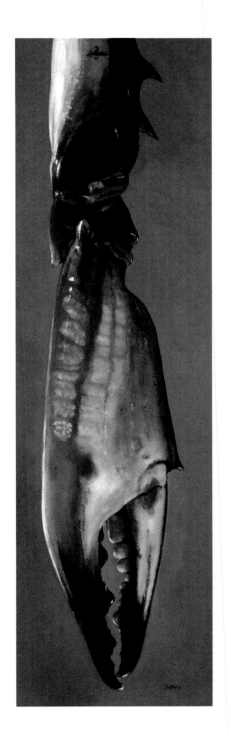

Acknowledgments

Some of my first memories connecting me to the coast start on a weathered pier on Davis Bayou.

I remember walking as a child at sunset under the canopy of giant live and sand oaks out to the old pier to dump a pot of scraps from Sunday dinner. The remains of my grandmother Unimay's cast-iron-fried chicken, her famous rice and gravy, and a myriad of stewed and pickled vegetables were swarmed over by what seemed like thousands of catfish as the sky darkened over the water. I remember this as if it were yesterday.

Those drives from Pascagoula to my grandparents' camp-style home at Eagle Point in Ocean Springs for Sunday supper in the 1970s are where I think my appreciation for the intimacy of great food and family at a common dinner table began.

My mother's parents lived three hours to the north, and while we didn't make it to just south of Jackson as often back then, those country dinners were also crucial to my upbringing and sense of family, as well as to my understanding of the state of Mississippi. Mouse, as I affectionately called my grandmother, was always relentlessly and masterfully baking her famous yeast rolls, teacakes, sugar cookies, and all sorts of pies for our visits—pecan being my favorite. Summer trips north of the coast as a kid were filled with picking vegetables for Mouse's dinners and adventures feeding her chickens—even the fearsome and prized rooster, Leroy Brown. Playing on the farm in that hot dirt with my momma and Mouse is one of my favorite childhood memories. Hurricane Katrina took Mouse's antique pie safe from me, but nothing can ever take away the memory of the smells or the taste of her yeast rolls or pecan pies—or maybe even the fear of that rooster, Leroy Brown.

My parents' kitchen was my favorite place growing up—we ate most meals and seemed to solve all of the world's problems there. The kitchen was the nucleus for our family, as it was for my parents during their childhoods. I cannot thank my mom and dad enough for inspiring me through their love, patience, and commitment to and support of my dreams. My parents showed me what a magical place a kitchen could be for creativity and love, and I aspire every day to pass that on to my two daughters.

I was blessed that my parents' best friends would eventually become my in-laws. I spent many years enjoying the meals cooked by the Taylors, and I will never be able to thank Austin and Ariel enough for feeding me and loving me like one of their own . . . and for allowing me a place in their kitchen to cook for them, every now and then.

There is a common thread here, not only in my acknowledgments, but throughout this book. One of love of food and family with kitchens and home taking center stage, something I understand so much more now and owe directly to my beautiful wife, Hanna—I cannot imagine an existence without you. I am inspired and driven further each day to pursue our ideas and dreams, all of which would be unobtainable without your amazing support and love! Thank you for tolerating the late nights during the progression of this book, including the often frustrated and misdirected antics of my coauthors and friends. It may have seemed unlikely at first that we were actually working when it involved boats and fires out on Horn Island with fresh-caught redfish cooking over hot coals—but we were!

Most importantly, though, to my daughters, Taylor and Bowen—my heart beats for you. I hope this book eventually gives you an incredible insight into your love- and food-driven family and into your home.

—Matthew Mayfield

Edgar Degas said, "Painting is easy when you don't know how, but very difficult when you do." I agree with that sentiment and have spent my adult life in the difficult pursuit of honestly learning the craft of paint.

I was raised on Mississippi's Gulf Coast by two loving parents who gave me a strong work ethic and all the support I needed to become an artist. Like all children, I drew. By fourth grade, when other children were discovering the joy of reading, I was finding it a chore. The retreat from my dyslexic agony of reading and writing propelled me into the visual world. Using the back of technical drawings my father would bring home from work, I spent countless hours drawing. My decision to become an artist was an easy one, but how to go about doing that was unknown. With no one else in my family having any real aptitude for the visual arts, I had difficulty finding people who knew the craft of painting.

So I went to college and had a great time, but I discovered that most of my professors didn't know how to draw or paint. It wasn't their fault. They were products of the 1950s and '60s, when abstract expressionism ruled and representational art was dead and buried. It was a world of artist-teachers teaching new artist-teachers how to reinvent the wheel—a wheel that everybody had forgotten how to make.

I moved to New Orleans after college, where I was introduced to the New Orleans Academy of Fine Arts and, more importantly, its founder, Auseklis Ozols. He understands and is able to teach the disciplines of painting and the virtues that come from the hard work of truly looking at the beauty that surrounds us. Like any complicated subject, the more you learn, the more there is to learn.

Now that I was beginning to understand the correct way to rub oily pigments onto canvas, I needed to decide what to paint. To paraphrase Mark Twain, you should "paint what you know," and I knew the Gulf Coast of Mississippi.

The home I grew up in looked out over the Mississippi Sound. From my backyard, we would explore those warm waters in small john boats and various little sailboats. We would fish for speckled trout and collect crabs and oysters. We took frequent trips to the lighthouse on Round Island and then farther out to Horn Island. My love of nature, obviously the most powerful theme in my artwork, was nurtured there.

I now live in New Orleans with my beautiful wife, Nici, and my incredible son, Enzo. The sky and its clouds are often my substitute for nature here in the city, supplemented by frequent trips back to Ocean Springs and the barrier islands.

I'll wrap this up with one more quote, from the artist whose passion for the natural world of the Mississippi Gulf Coast has inspired so many: Walter Anderson. "The first poetry is written against the wind by sailors and farmers who sing with the wind in their teeth. The second poetry is written by scholars and wine drinkers who learned to know a good thing. The third poetry is sometimes never written but when it is it is by those who have brought nature and art together into one thing."

—Billy Solitario

Working on this book has allowed me to rediscover and dig deeper into a Mississippi Coast that I already knew and loved. I often think back to those nights in the 1980s on the second floor of my dorm at St. Stanislaus when I would quietly sit in the window, craning out to look towards the bay. I'd smoke cigarettes deep into the night, the light snores of my two roommates interrupted only by the horns of the trains crossing the bay bridge. Those long nights in my dorm-room window as a teenager have achieved a sort of mythical proportion in my head, but they definitely branded me with a love for the coast.

Today, the Mississippi Coast has truly become a second home for me again and is a place full of old friends and new ones who easily feel to me as if I've known them my entire life. I am indebted for all of these friendships and want to thank everyone who contributed recipes, ideas, or time towards the completion of this book—I hope that you are as proud of it as we are and had as much fun putting it together as we did.

Specifically I'd like to thank John George DeRussy for our friendship of many years. John George first showed me the beauty and the bounty of the Mississippi Coast from his family's camp on White's Bayou in Pearlington. We had many crazy weekends and great pirogue expeditions out there as teenagers—I can still name every tributary of the Pearl River (in order from west to east). Thank you also to Stacey Meyer of New Orleans and Mary Hewes of Gulfport for their proofreading, recipes, and dear friendships; and our editor, Nina Kooij, production manager, Jeff Hench, publisher, Kathleen Calhoun Nettleton, and everyone at Pelican Publishing for recognizing the value of this book and for working with us to help share and celebrate the beauty, culture, and food of the Mississippi Coast. Thanks to the talented New Orleans photographer Chris Granger, whom I finally ran into in Havana, Cuba after sailing in the first major regatta from the U.S. to that island nation in late 2015. His photographic contributions added a whole other dimension to this book, and I look forward to working with him on future projects.

I wish to thank the Mayfields and Taylors of Ocean Springs, who have been and are always incredibly generous with their hospitality and their family stories and recipes—I am honored to call them extended family. Thanks to Hanna Mayfield for keeping her husband focused and for putting up with our antics when we weren't so focused. I'd also like to acknowledge the 48-foot Hatteras, the *Miz Mendy IV*—most of this book was concocted and typed onboard in every season, on runs out to Horn Island or docked in the Ocean Springs Harbor, over the slow course of three years.

I'd also like to dearly thank my parents, sister, and her family for always supporting me in all of my long projects, especially my mother. With our French ancestors that reach back to the 17th century in South Louisiana and her Cajun upbringing along the levee in Gramercy, she raised me to know the legacy of good food. One of the great comforts in my life is knowing that I have a container of her gumbo or red beans (or both) in my freezer.

And finally, to the two goofballs whom I can now call coauthors: it only took me about 12 hours into an expedition to Horn Island on assignment for *BoatU.S. Magazine* with two strangers for the idea to take hold. We had a classically trained chef, a very talented artist, and a writer boating around and telling each other so many stories and tall tales that by the time we had a fire going at sunset on the beach, I knew not only that we were kindred spirits, but that we had a story to tell— together. I think I first broached the subject of a book near the Flats on Horn while we dragged most of an enormous waterlogged tree trunk, at Matthew's insistence, nearly a quarter-mile up the shoreline to feed the fire late in the night. I know for sure that I explained to Matthew and Billy, as we motored back to Ocean Springs the next morning, that if we did this book, we would always be connected. It's a good thing that I now consider them both to be best friends of mine. (Nate, that man about town in Ocean Springs, was also out there on a trip or two.)

Now let's fire up the old Hatteras and celebrate out on Horn Island. I still have a bottle of smuggled Cuban rum left, and we promised a few people who helped make this book possible that we'd sabre a magnum or two of chilled Veuve Clicquot out on the island, by a driftwood fire.

—Troy Gilbert

Solitario

Introduction

There's a certain sound to the Mississippi Coast, whether you are sitting on a porch and listening to the trains cross the bays and bayous with their horns fading into the distance or standing a few steps inland on the east end of Horn Island, where the white sand burns your bare feet. You hear it as the men and women clean fish on the piers and tell their tall tales, and you hear it as the church bells ring down the main streets and the kids run off to the parks to muss up their Sunday clothes. It's there as the evening falls and the cast nets strike the water and the shrimp boats head out into the Sound. There's the sound of cheers when the Bulldogs or sometimes even the Rebels score, and there's the sound of high winds and high waters. Mostly, though, you hear the sounds of boat engines, trawlers, and bows slicing through water; the wind through the oaks and pines on the shore; and the laughter of friends and family—and their cooking. Always there are the sounds from the kitchens and grills and crab pots, with their fires started and letting everyone know they aren't company, but home.

The Mississippi Coast is one of those forgotten coastlines on the Gulf of Mexico, short in stature but with a history and culinary line that is more robust and diverse than almost anywhere else on the Gulf Coast. Mixing the interior Mississippi Delta cooking and the abundance of the state's crops with the bounty of the Mississippi Sound—and then, for added measure, influence from the French and New Orleans—the coast has always found its own way.

On the Coast is a celebration of the sleepy little Mississippi Gulf Coast towns, with their well-used porch swings filled with neighbors chatting and laughing as condensation drips from their grandmothers' heirloom crystal rocks glasses, and all the while the cicadas calling out from the deep Southern evenings. It showcases the art inspired by white sand spilling and shifting from the beaches onto roads shaded by sprawling 200-year-old oaks that easily outnumber the citizens. But above all, it serves to highlight the culture, food, and people who live along the coast, where Walker Percy characters took daytrips, and the barrier islands to the south, where William Faulkner and Eudora Welty sailed on occasion.

Down here, all roads lead to the coast.

The Mississippi Sound, the Gulf of Mexico, and the coast's bays and bayous hold incredibly fertile oyster beds, shrimping grounds, and diverse fishing that are all protected by a run of small, sandy, barrier islands that make up the Gulf Islands National Seashore. Located a quick cruise offshore, these islands are home to the remnants of massive Civil War-era forts and were notoriously used by pirates, privateers, and smugglers throughout most of their history, as well as by the British and the Yankees as staging grounds for their invasions of New Orleans. This is a coast whose history and descendants still live on the waters traversed by French and Spanish explorers and Native Americans not that many generations ago. Many of the locals hold that lineage and have their family's oral history to prove it, and these men and women still ply the waters of the Mississippi Sound and the Gulf, albeit now for a different bounty—blue crab, shrimp, and oysters.

Many of the coastal towns, such as Ocean Springs and Bay St. Louis, have become art communities, full of Southern characters. Like the cowboy poets of the West, it's not uncommon to see beat-up old trucks with fishing poles on the rear-window gun racks and stacks of finished canvases on the passenger seat, along with a black lab or two in the stern. Take the time to chat with the locals. It's likely you're talking with a descendant of the only president of the Confederacy, or a renowned artist inspired by Walter Anderson, or a charter captain whose family arrived with the French or Spanish 300 years ago. You are in the Deep South, where hospitality is as natural as breathing.

On lazy afternoons, the porches and verandas come alive on the coast as the cooling breeze blows off the Sound. Sailors gather on the decks of the yacht clubs to drink cocktails and share their adventures on the water, as many have been doing at clubs that were founded in the 1800s and are counted among the oldest in not only the United States, but the Western Hemisphere. The coast has a long history under sail, one that transitioned from transportation and utility to recreation in the early 20th century, and onboard these boats, amateur and expert crews revel in the hours spent on the water. As the sun falls and meals are roused from the galley below, stories and laughter are shared, and all the while the spray coming off the bow becomes saltier and the lights from the cities and towns vanish as they quietly sail along the Gulf Islands—as they have been doing for generations.

The balconies and tables at restaurants throughout the coast fill early as the sun sets. Locals sip on Southern Pecan Nut Brown Ale from Lazy Magnolia, one

ON THE COAST

of the local breweries, while awaiting their dishes featuring seafood landed earlier that day. Throughout the revitalizing downtowns of Gulfport and Biloxi, or overlooking the marinas of Bay St. Louis, Pass Christian, and Long Beach, diners enjoy their meals while watching the shrimp boats and oystermen unloading their hauls next to old Biloxi schooners and luggers. On family piers out at Eagle Point or Sandy Hook, men and women whose lives are defined by the water set up boilers and empty their crab traps, or shuck those beautiful oysters or "rocks" and toss them on the grill drizzled with butter, spices, and garlic.

This is a coast that wouldn't know how to get together with friends and family without cooking—it's just what you do. The kitchen or the grill or the crawfish pot is where the action is. It's the time to enjoy the fruits from the mornings out on the water or after hunting the piney woods for deer in the early cool days of the fall.

Three hundred years after their founding, these idyllic towns and their people are waiting for you to join them and listen to the Southern twilight on the bays, to relax on an old wooden deck surrounded by gardens of azaleas, plumbago, and centuries-old oak trees, with white sand brushing at your feet as the breeze lifts off the Sound and the condensation drips down your crystal rocks glass.

The Biloxi Light Station in 1892. (Photograph courtesy of the United States Coast Guard)

Even the ospreys know to demand fresh Mississippi shrimp.

Boat Snacks

Aunt Ginnie's Cheese Straws

Recipe courtesy of Virginia Mosby Hewes Spotswood
Yield: 12 servings

Any fine young lady from Mississippi knows better than to travel without cheese straws and her pearls.

1 pound Mississippi State University extra-sharp cheddar cheese, grated	2 teaspoons cayenne pepper
	2 teaspoons paprika
	1 cup butter
2 cups all-purpose flour	2 tablespoons cold water
1½ teaspoons salt	

Transfer cheese to a large mixing bowl and allow to come to room temperature. In a separate bowl, combine the flour, salt, cayenne pepper, and paprika and sift—twice. Melt the butter and pour it over the grated cheese. Add the flour to the cheese and butter mixture along with the water and work together. When ready, the cheese "dough" will be smooth. Put the dough into a pastry bag and squeeze out thin, 3-inch lengths onto waxed paper on a baking sheet. Preheat the oven to 350 degrees. Bake for 15 minutes or until the straws are lightly browned on top and a bit darker on the bottom. Transfer to a rack and let cool. Serve immediately or store in a resealable container for up to 1 week.

 Chef's Note: For a bit of an extra kick, stir in a teaspoon or two of Sriracha or your favorite hot sauce.

Coast "Chex" Mix

Recipe courtesy of Mary Hewes
Yield: 12 servings

The old Biloxi lugger Vanalburt-Lee *has been in the Hewes family since the 1940s, and expeditions out to the Gulf Islands have given rise to certain food traditions in the family. This easy "Chex" mix from Ms. Mary is an ideal boat snack. The saltiness of your pruned fingers after hours of floating and swimming in the Sound only adds to the flavor.*

8 tablespoons butter
2 tablespoons Worcestershire sauce
2 teaspoons Tabasco or Crystal hot
   sauce
3 cups puffed rice cereal,
   unsweetened
3 cups shredded wheat cereal,
   unsweetened
3 cups cornflakes cereal,
   unsweetened

2 cups peanuts, unsalted
2 cups pecan halves
2 cups almonds
1 cup cashews
2 cups pretzel sticks
1½ teaspoons garlic powder
1½ teaspoons onion powder
2 teaspoons cayenne pepper
Cajun seasoning to taste (be heavy
   handed)

Preheat the oven to 250 degrees. Add the butter to a baking pan and let melt in the oven. Remove, add the Worcestershire and hot sauce, and mix well with a spatula. Then add the cereals, nuts, and pretzel sticks, coating well with the butter and Worcestershire sauce by mixing around. Sprinkle with the garlic and onion powder, cayenne pepper, and Cajun seasoning. Return to the oven and bake for 30 minutes. Every 10 minutes or so, turn the mix in the baking sheet and return to the oven. Remove from the oven and allow to cool. Transfer to a large resealable plastic container or bags. The mix can be stored for at least 2 weeks.

The Biloxi lugger Vanalburt-Lee *heads south on an expedition.*

Hurricane Hole Pimento Cheese

Recipe courtesy of Dr. Austin Taylor
Yield: 10 to 12 servings

The heat of this pimento cheese can be adjusted as desired. Consider adding splashes of Sriracha or your favorite hot sauce.

8 ounces Mississippi State University sharp cheddar cheese, coarsely grated
8 ounces Mississippi State University extra-sharp cheddar cheese, coarsely grated
4 ounces cream cheese

1 4-ounce bottle chopped pimentos, undrained
¾ cup Duke's or store-bought mayonnaise
½ tablespoon onion powder
½ tablespoon garlic powder
½ tablespoon black pepper

Mix the coarsely grated cheese with the cream cheese in a mixing bowl. Add the remaining ingredients and thoroughly mix. More or less mayonnaise may be used, according to desired consistency. Serve immediately with minced green and/or red onions as garnish and with fancy crackers or transfer to a resealable container for storage. The pimento cheese can be stored in the refrigerator for up to 2 weeks.

Back Bay Boiled Peanuts

Yield: 12 servings

Don't be afraid . . . give in to your impending boiled-peanut addiction.

5 pounds peanuts in shell, raw
1 cup kosher salt
1 4-ounce bottle Zatarain's liquid
   crab boil
Water to cover

Wash the peanuts and place them in a large pot. Add the salt and crab boil and cover with water. Heat the pot and boil for 1 hour. Remove from heat and allow to rest in the water for 1 hour. Remove a single peanut to cool for sampling. When ready, the peanuts should be soft, juicy, and very salty. Add more salt to the water if needed and, if necessary, boil for another 30 minutes. Remove from heat and allow the peanuts to cool and soak in the water for another 30 minutes. Remove from the water and serve.

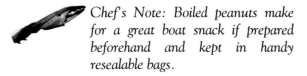 *Chef's Note: Boiled peanuts make for a great boat snack if prepared beforehand and kept in handy resealable bags.*

Spicy Boiled-Peanut "Hummus" Spread

Yield: 2 cups

2 cups shelled boiled peanuts
¼ cup coarsely chopped green
   onions
¼ cup crumbled feta cheese
4 cloves garlic, coarsely chopped

1 tablespoon lemon juice
1 tablespoon Greek seasoning
1 teaspoon black pepper
4 tablespoons extra-virgin olive oil

Place all ingredients except the olive oil in the bowl of a food processor. Pulse several times, then add the olive oil in a slow, steady stream while the processor is running. Process until the mixture is smooth. Transfer to a serving bowl and serve with your favorite fancy crackers or wedges of pita bread.

Jalapeno Cornbread with Cracklins

Yield: 8 to 10 servings

This is delicious either hot or cold, but it is much better prepared in advance and enjoyed while anchored on the north side of Horn Island after a successful morning of fishing.

1 cup Original Grit Girl cornmeal
½ teaspoon salt
1 teaspoon baking soda
2 eggs, beaten
½ cup buttermilk
1 cup creamed corn
1 cup cubed Mississippi State
   University cheddar cheese

3 small jalapenos, seeded and
   chopped
1 cup cooked, coarsely chopped
   cracklins or bacon
¼ cup vegetable oil
3 pats butter

Preheat the oven to 350 degrees. In a large mixing bowl, combine the cornmeal, salt, and baking powder. Add the eggs and buttermilk and thoroughly mix together to form a smooth batter. Add the remaining ingredients except for the oil and butter, and mix well. Grease a large cast-iron skillet with the oil. Pour the batter into the skillet and transfer it to the oven. Bake for 30 minutes or until done when tested with a toothpick. Carefully remove from oven and, while it cools, put butter on top and spread around. Cut into wedges when it is cool. Wrap each wedge in a paper towel, and store together in a resealable bag.

 Chef's Note: The best cracklins can be found at many gas stations throughout southern Mississippi and Louisiana's Cajun Country or at your local butcher shop.

Wolf River Egg Salad with Pimento Cheese Finger Sandwiches

Yield: 20 servings

In the old days, wives and mothers would store these lunches in shoeboxes and the men would keep them secure and dry onboard.

1 serving Wolf River Egg Salad (see index)
1 serving Hurricane Hole Pimento Cheese (see above)
1 loaf white bread, sliced

In a large mixing bowl, thoroughly combine the prepared egg salad and pimento-cheese dip. Spread some of the mixture thickly onto 1 slice of bread. Cover with another slice of bread and cut into quarters. Repeat with remaining ingredients and seal in a resealable plastic container. Keep chilled on ice.

Deviled Eggs with Blue Crab and Apple-Smoked Bacon

Yield: 12 servings

12 hard-boiled eggs
1 tablespoon minced red onion
1 teaspoon capers
1 tablespoon minced celery
1 tablespoon minced red bell pepper
½ cup homemade or store-bought
   mayonnaise
½ tablespoon Creole mustard
1 tablespoon chopped parsley

Juice of ½ lemon
1 tablespoon Sriracha
¼ cup sweet pickle relish
Salt and pepper to taste
¼ pint fresh Mississippi lump blue
   crabmeat, twice picked
4 slices cooked apple-smoked
   bacon, crumbled

Peel and slice the eggs in half lengthwise, remove the yolks, and set aside. Place the red onion, capers, celery, and red bell pepper in the bowl of a food processor and pulse until roughly diced together. Carefully drain off any extra liquid. In a large mixing bowl, thoroughly combine the egg yolks, vegetable mixture, mayonnaise, mustard, parsley, lemon juice, Sriracha, pickle relish, and salt and pepper. Place the blended mixture into a pastry bag and pipe into the egg whites. Garnish each with crabmeat and a crumble of bacon. Serve immediately or keep chilled in a sealed container in an ice chest for a day's fishing.

Smoked Ham Dip

Yield: 10 to 12 servings

This dip would also make a fantastic filling for deviled eggs, with each topped with a touch of pickle relish. Simply mix the hard-boiled yolks into the dip and stuff the egg halves.

4 cups cubed smoked ham
1 cup garlic dill pickles
1 small onion, coarsely chopped
1 cup homemade or store-bought
   mayonnaise
1 tablespoon sour cream

1 teaspoon Pickapeppa Sauce
1 teaspoon yellow mustard
2 teaspoons cayenne pepper
2 teaspoons black pepper
1 teaspoon salt
1 tablespoon Uncle Duke's Geaux Jus*

Combine all ingredients together in a food processor and blend fully. Transfer the dip to a large serving bowl and serve with fancy crackers, topped with pickle relish.

*See "Resources" chapter

Smoked Mullet and Jalapeno Dip

Yield: 12 servings

This is a great dip to keep secure in an ice chest with the cold drinks and break out for an afternoon snack, served with fancy crackers from a box.

Hickory chips
9 filets mullet with skin, about 3 pounds
2 cups sour cream
2 cups homemade or store-bought mayonnaise
4 ounces feta cheese
1 cup pickled jalapenos, minced
½ bunch green onions, diced
2 tablespoons lemon juice
Bonney's or your favorite hot sauce to taste
4 slices apple-smoked bacon, cooked and crumbled
1 tablespoon garlic salt
Kosher salt and fresh-ground black pepper to taste

Preheat a ceramic smoker to 250 degrees. Once the smoker is hot, add the hickory chips. Carefully line the grill of the smoker with aluminum foil. When the chips begin to smoke, lay the mullet filets, skin side down, on the aluminum foil. Smoke the filets for 20 to 25 minutes.

Remove the filets from the smoker and, using a fork, flake the fish into a large mixing bowl. Discard the skin. Add the remaining ingredients to the bowl and mix well. Transfer the dip to a resealable container and refrigerate for at least 4 hours before serving. The refrigerated dip can be stored for up to 4 days.

Atomic Pelican Beaks

Yield: 8 servings

8 jalapenos, halved and seeded
1 package cream cheese, room
   temperature

1 tube Jimmy Dean sausage
1 pound thin-sliced bacon

Preheat the grill to 350 degrees. Fill each jalapeno half with cream cheese. Fold a spoonful of the Jimmy Dean sausage into a little football shape and place into the cream-cheese stuffing in each jalapeno. Wrap each with 1 slice bacon and secure with a toothpick. Grill for 30 minutes or until bacon is done. Serve immediately or store in a resealable container in the refrigerator for up to 1 week.

The coast calendar is always full with festivals, art walks, and parades, and residents don't ever mind sharing what's cooking.

Oysters in a Pinch

Yield: 4 servings

We've all been there—pulling fish into the boat like crazy and the crew has already consumed everything onboard. A wise boat captain always keeps a few tins of oysters onboard for emergency snacks.

1 tin Reese's medium or petite
   oysters
1 box fancy crackers

1 jalapeno, minced
Bonney's or Crystal hot sauce

For each serving, place 1 or 2 oysters on your favorite fancy cracker. Dribble a bit of the minced jalapeno onto the oyster and drizzle on hot sauce. Enjoy!

 Chef's Note: It's nice to have one guy fix the oyster crackers for the crew and then hand them out while the rest are engaged in fishing.

An Expedition to the Gulf Islands

Such a sky—such water, and Horn Island
between with me walking it . . .
—Walter Inglis Anderson

Faulkner sailed them, as did the pirate Jean Lafitte. They were the first islands Jimmy Buffett knew and dreamt of as a kid in Pascagoula and the muse for the art of Walter Anderson displayed in the Smithsonian. Mississippi's Gulf Islands were the rallying point for 60 British frigates prior to their failed invasion of New Orleans, and like then, seeds and tropical driftwoods still push north from the Caribbean and South America onto their sugar-sand beaches.

Once home to a litany of pirates, Confederate gunrunners, and 1970s drug smugglers, Mississippi's barrier islands are today uninhabited and quiet, with Cuba and Mexico the nearest landfall south. Visited mainly by locals looking for good fishing or overnight beach camping, these sandy spits of dunes and lagoons are wholly protected as a national seashore and wildlife preserve and stunning in their beauty and history.

Stringing along the entire coast of Mississippi, these long and narrow islands—Cat, Ship, Horn, Sand, and Petit Bois—are an important first line of defense for the state from hurricanes. Forming the boundary between the Gulf of Mexico and the Mississippi Sound, they are located 7 to 12 miles offshore of quaint, historic coastal towns offering everything from antiquing to casinos and are an unheralded and forgotten cruising ground.

Due east lie Alabama's developed barrier islands and the heavily trafficked waters of the panhandle of Florida, but cruisers rarely take the time to travel the few extra miles. Except for serving as daytrip or regatta destinations from the coast or New Orleans, the islands are skirted by shrimp boats and oystermen plying the Sound and not much else. Locals will tell you with their wry Mississippi accent that the Gulf Coast does not end at the farthest point west that tourists can toss a mullet at the legendary Flora-Bama bar.

Lugging 40-pound bags of ice from the pink bait shop in Ocean Springs and onto the 48-foot Hatteras and 21-foot Boston whaler for use as scat boat, Chef Matthew Mayfield and coastal artist Billy Solitario needle each other as they have done since their childhood.

"So, Matthew, are you a fisherman?"

"Well, I don't know, Billy. What constitutes a fisherman?"

"I don't know. Do you consider yourself one?"

"Well, I fish. What constitutes an artist?"

The reality is that these two grew up together on the Mississippi Coast, running these barrier islands. This was their childhood playground, and now it is their professional inspiration. Mayfield is a classically trained chef from the Culinary Institute of America and Solitario is a renowned artist with a studio in nearby New Orleans. I join them and we watch as Dr. Bob Thomas, the director of the environmental program at Loyola University, and James Beard-nominated filmmaker Kevin McCaffrey arrive from New Orleans. They unpack their cameras and gear and pass it all to us down the piers rebuilt after Hurricane Katrina. We are headed out on an expedition to explore, document, and enjoy these barrier islands that are vanishing into the Gulf of Mexico.

While the new arrivals secure bunks in the Hatteras, the hometown guys joke on the dock with the shrimpers and charter captains who are already off of work from their early-morning trawling. These are men and women who, if they were coastal oaks with their roots deep in the salt and dusted by white sand, you could figure their age by the big storms they have weathered. This marina is a small world in a small town on a coast that has endured everything.

Rising on a slight bluff, Ocean Springs was relatively spared from most of the cataclysmic destruction from the hurricane in 2005, its historic downtown and neighborhoods left intact. Today it is quietly booming, with the feel of an Austin, Texas in its infancy. Only blocks from the marina, Government Street is growing into a music and restaurant scene. Home to Walter Anderson's legacy and

Part of the Gulf Islands National Seashore, Horn Island is known for her unmistakable beauty and as the muse for artist Walter Anderson.

Shearwater Pottery, Ocean Springs has always been an arts town and it is finally being discovered.

The Hatteras casts off, and McCaffrey films footage of the big boat as he follows in the whaler helmed by Nate, a local man about town and friend of the guys from the coast. Across the entrance to the back bay as we convoy southeast, high-rise hotels and their casinos command the beachfront in Biloxi, a different world from genteel Ocean Springs with her beachfront dotted with private homes and the Ocean Springs Yacht Club.

Cruising south from anywhere on the Gulf Coast always feels like heading north for some reason, and Horn Island rises low on the horizon. It doesn't appear to be much on the approach—only 14 miles long and a quarter-mile wide, with several outcroppings of dunes, pines, and oak trees. We slide in at the "fat" west end of Horn. There is almost pure beach on three sides, and these are not the Atlantic beaches of Florida or Jersey—these are Gulf Coast beaches. Giant sandy swaths easily reach out 25 yards in each direction, with lee coves populated by brown pelicans, ospreys, and a myriad of other seabirds, startled only by periodic redfish runs in the shallows. Surf pounds the southern shore, while the north can be as quiet as a Pennsylvania Amish pond, but with water temperatures averaging above 80 degrees in the summer and 60 degrees in the deep winter.

Solitario's career as an artist was made when he started painting these island scenes, and he's obviously ready to dig his toes into the sand. He wants to paint but mostly talks of redfish and wading for oysters at the mouth of the inner lagoons. Mayfield wants to boat. He's the skipper, and we round Horn Island to the south. At the eastern point is a secluded shoreline, and no one is concerned that anyone will be there. There is an unwritten rule that each island is claimed by the coastal town that lies due north. Bay St. Louis, Pass Christian, and Gulfport get Cat and Ship; Biloxi and Ocean Springs get Horn; and

Horn Island rises in the distance beyond a buoy marking the channel.

Pascagoula and Gautier have Petit Bois. With the prevailing winds and currents tending to be from the east, the western cove of Horn can be heavily used by locals on weekends as a lee shore, especially if a strong easterly is at play, but we have light winds.

The eastern shore of Horn is magical. The Gulf of Mexico crashing a stone's throw to the south is a close white noise behind the dunes that rise 20 feet. Their perfect crystalline quartz sand that thousands of years ago washed down from the Appalachians rests here now for rabbit and ghost-crab footprints—and ours. Solitario sets up his easel almost immediately in the pine straw and sand beneath a run of pine trees that are home to massive osprey nests. The chef and biologist walk down the beach discussing foraging on the island, while McCaffrey sets up his HD camera and starts filming. Nate cracks open a beverage on the whaler as I walk off and explore the dunes for sun-bleached driftwood for tonight's campfire.

Only a few steps inland, it seems as if everything is left behind and you are alone. A distant squall throws off lightning, and my feet dig deep into the white sand. Amazed that there are no human footprints here, I feel something that ancient explorers likely never felt—guilt. But I walk on, tracking up a small rise, and find a quiet lagoon. The brackish pond fed by freshwater springs and rainfall is lined with reeds on one side and the dunes I now stand on. I disturb some more rabbit footprints until the dunes and light scrub give way to the pink and black sand of the flats, peppered with thousands of seashell shards. When I find the beach, the Gulf of Mexico is rolling as a tropical breeze freshens from the south. We are likely the only people on this island.

With years of childhood experience that makes them fearless, Mayfield and Solitario break out a paddleboard and fish one of the inner lagoons known to house redfish and a stray alligator or two. Standing on the dunes, watching and waiting for their inevitable death that never comes, the rest of us discuss the unbelievable survival of the island's rabbits and raccoons in the 30-foot storm surge that covered this island years ago. It is mystifying even to the biologist.

By campfire, the shadows play on the dunes and the Mississippi Coast is quiet in her distant lights while Mayfield cooks a simple dish of redfish in the coals. The Sound washes on the shore and a few shrimp boats slide past periodically. The discussion turns to the single park ranger who has lived on Horn Island for the last 20 years and how his world could not be that dissimilar from Edward Abbey's experience in the deserts of Utah.

On the Gulf beach in the morning, the surf is salty and warm and we prepare to move on. Only a few miles to the west lies Ship Island, with her massive Civil War fortress that still guards the coast. The North quickly conquered Ship Island in 1861 and turned the fort into a prison camp for Confederates. The island's natural harbor was then used again as a staging point for the capture of New Orleans, the Union Navy succeeding where the British Navy failed some 50 years earlier. The fort and beaches make Ship Island of interest to tourists who arrive daily via charters from nearby Gulfport, and while excellent anchorages abound, it does not have the remote, quiet feel of the other islands until after dusk.

The entire coastline of Mississippi is populated by transient-friendly yacht clubs, including three of the five oldest clubs in the United States as well as $94 million in new state-of-the-art marinas since 2005. The Gulfport Small Craft Harbor is a good resupply or overnight destination, and the marina can accommodate vessels up to 140 feet. The Gulfport Yacht Club as well as restaurants and bars are located only three blocks away in downtown Gulfport.

Scrub pines throw shadows as the sun sets.

ON THE COAST

Another quick run from the coast is Cat Island, originally named Isle aux Chats for the multitude of raccoons on the island that French explorers mistakenly identified as cats. Unlike the narrow and long shape of the rest of the barrier islands, it is *T* shaped. White-sand beaches, palmettos, pines, and oaks also abound here, but the southwestern cove of the island is pure marsh and swamp. Overnight camping is allowed, although a small interior portion is still privately owned and posted. From the beaches of Cat Island, the transformation to the marshy coastline of Louisiana becomes visible as the water turns darker with the influx of the muddy water from the mouth of the Mississippi River and her bays. Continue on a few miles to the south and the eroding Louisiana barrier islands of the Chandeleurs await, while to the northwest, the deepwater Rigolets Pass opens up and leads into Lake Pontchartrain and then New Orleans' marina district of West End.

Only eight miles north of Cat Island lie Bay St. Louis and her namesake town, the perfect bookend for any Gulf Island expedition, with her quiet oak-lined streets, waterfront seafood restaurants, antique shops, and history dating back to French explorers in 1699.

With their architectural history mostly spared by Hurricane Katrina, Bay St. Louis and Ocean Springs have been thrust into the vanguard of a coast that's still searching for its identity after the storm. Each of us onboard the Hatteras lost something in 2005, and we understand that as we motor back home and to our cars. It's one thing to look on a map or read a newspaper story and distantly understand the importance of these islands, but "it is another thing to dig your feet into the sand and hear those nesting seabirds and really get that these islands are not only here to protect us, my family, the casinos, or an oil and gas refinery but that there is an important relationship here," Mayfield explains. "We have to help them protect us."

In one of those thick Southern skies where you can truly feel the height of the atmosphere above, the sun sets and the islands' shores sparkle in crazy reds and purples. But after only a mile of heading back north, the islands again become quiet, plain, and then vanish. They are real magic hidden in plain sight, waiting to be explored.

Right: Ship Island in 1853, 1892, and 1954. (Photographs courtesy of the United States Coast Guard)

Starters

Solitario

Vancleave Micro-Specials with Garlic Aioli

Yield: 12 servings

According to coast lore, C. L. "Kip" Dees of Vancleave invented the "Vancleave Special" in 1947. A frequent patron of Rosetti's Café on Howard Avenue in Biloxi, Kip requested that cheese be added to his regular crabmeat po' boy. The owner of Rosetti's became fond of the sandwich, and this special eventually became the most expensive item on the menu at $1.75.

However, there is another version of the tale. In 1941, a young Vertis Ramsay, who would go on to become the circuit clerk for Jackson County, regularly stopped in for lunch at Rosetti's. He was known for requesting that cheese be melted onto his crabmeat po' boy, and as we all know, 1941 is a full six years before 1947.

1 egg yolk
1½ tablespoons minced garlic
2 tablespoons water
1 teaspoon lemon juice
1 tablespoon extra-virgin olive oil
Salt and pepper to taste
¼ cup diced red onions

Cajun seasoning to taste
1 pint fresh Mississippi lump blue
   crabmeat, twice picked
12 pistolettes
½ pound Mississippi State University
   cheddar cheese, thinly sliced

Vancleave Specials reinvented as sliders and served with a fresh salad make for an easy and delicious snack for guests.

Preheat the oven to 400 degrees. Combine the egg yolk, garlic, water, and lemon juice in a small bowl. If necessary, secure the bowl on the work surface by placing it on a damp kitchen towel. Slowly drizzle in the olive oil with one hand, while vigorously whisking with the other to form an emulsion. Add the salt and pepper, red onions, seasoning, and crabmeat and fold gently to combine.

Slice the pistolettes in half lengthwise and place the halves split side up on a baking sheet. Place a medium-size spoonful of the blue-crab mixture on the pistolette bottoms. Then lay an even amount of sliced cheddar cheese on top of the crabmeat. Bake for 10 minutes or until the cheese is very bubbly. Remove from the oven and dust the cheese with Cajun seasoning or paprika and black pepper. Place the tops on the bottoms and transfer to a serving tray.

ON THE COAST

Panko-Fried Shrimp and Pimento-Cheese Hushpuppies

Yield: 6 to 8 servings

The trick to these is placing them in the freezer for just the right amount of time before frying. If they become too hardened, they will still be cold in the center after frying. It may take a few test runs to get these perfect, but it's well worth it!

1 cup Hurricane Hole Pimento
  Cheese (see index)
1 cup shrimp, boiled and coarsely
  chopped
½ cup thinly sliced green onions
Olive oil for frying

1 cup all-purpose flour or Zatarain's
  fish fry
2 eggs
½ cup half-and-half
1 box panko breadcrumbs
Comeback Sauce (see index)

Add the pimento cheese, boiled shrimp, and green onions to a mixing bowl and mix together well. Form into balls about the size of a hushpuppy, 1½ inches in diameter, and place on a tray. Place the tray in the freezer until balls are very firm but not frozen. A good rule of thumb is about 20 minutes, although this will vary depending on individual freezer settings and sizes.

Pour oil into a deep fryer and heat to 350 degrees. Place the flour in a shallow bowl. In another shallow bowl, whisk together the eggs and half-and-half. Place the panko in a third shallow bowl.

Dredge the balls in the flour and shake off the excess. Then dip into the egg wash and dredge in the panko. Using tongs, carefully place the balls in the fryer and cook until they turn golden brown, about 2 to 3 minutes. Try to keep them from touching as much as possible. Remove them with a slotted spoon and drain on a paper-towel-lined plate. Serve immediately with the sauce for dipping.

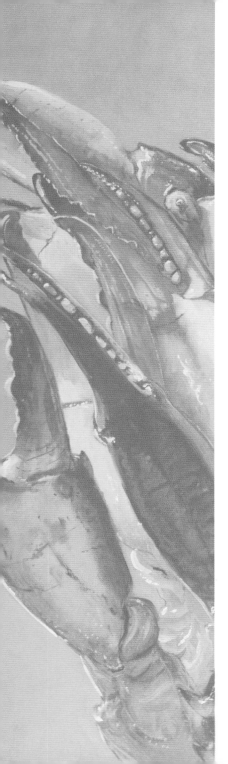

Shrimp Bread

Recipe courtesy of Ron Spiegel
Yield: 6 to 8 servings

This dish is a winner at parties and can be prepared early and refrigerated. To reheat, allow to come to room temperature before placing in the oven.

1 pound large round bread, either sourdough or French
3 large cloves garlic, minced
1 bunch green onions, diced
½ cup parsley, finely chopped
8 tablespoons unsalted butter, softened

2 tablespoons Ricard or Pernod
Salt and pepper
Cajun seasoning to taste
1 cup mushrooms, diced
1 pound fresh Mississippi shrimp, peeled and deveined
1 tablespoon white wine

Preheat oven to 400 degrees. Slice off the top of the bread and set aside. Hollow out the remaining bread, leaving a sizeable amount of bread to maintain structural integrity. Finely grind the removed bread in a food processor and set aside.

In a separate bowl, blend the garlic, green onions, parsley, butter, Ricard, 1 teaspoon salt, ½ teaspoon pepper, and Cajun seasoning until smooth. Spread ⅓ of the mixture on the bottom of the bread bowl, and then add the mushrooms. Add half of the shrimp and sprinkle lightly with salt and pepper.

Spread ⅓ of the butter mixture on top of the shrimp, and then add half of the ground bread. Follow with of the remaining shrimp and dust lightly with salt and pepper. Spread the final third of the butter mixture on top and then the remaining ground bread.

Drizzle the top layer with the wine. Bake for 25 to 30 minutes. When the bread becomes nicely browned, add the top "lid" of the bread and allow to cook for another 5 minutes. Serve on a platter.

Biloxi Doughnuts

Recipe courtesy of Micky Bradley
Yield: 6 servings

6 extra-large fresh Mississippi brown
   shrimp, peeled and deveined
2 teaspoons white pepper
2 teaspoons garlic salt
1 cup all-purpose flour
2 eggs
½ cup half-and-half

1 box Zatarain's or other seasoned
   fish fry
8 tablespoons butter
2 tablespoons extra-virgin olive oil
1 pint fresh Mississippi oysters
Pinch of sweet paprika
1 lemon, cut in 6 wedges

With a sharp knife, make an incision, lengthwise, through the back of each shrimp, being careful to leave the shrimp connected at the head and tail. Flatten the shrimp out to make a "doughnut" and season with the white pepper and garlic salt. Set aside.

Place the flour in a shallow bowl. In another shallow bowl, whisk together the eggs and half-and-half. Place the fish fry in a third shallow bowl.

In a skillet over medium-high heat, add the butter and just enough olive oil to cover the surface of the pan. Melt the butter. Dredge the shrimp in the flour and shake off the excess. Then dip into the egg wash, and dredge in the fish fry. Place in the skillet and cook until they turn golden brown on all sides. Use the same process for each of the oysters.

To serve, place the shrimp on a plate, dust with paprika, then drizzle some of the olive oil-butter sauce from the skillet on top. Finish by placing a fried oyster into each "doughnut" hole, add a lemon wedge to garnish, and serve.

Variants of the quaint Biloxi Cottage are common throughout the Mississippi Coast. They are somewhat similar to the shotgun houses of New Orleans.

Artichokes with Oyster Sauce

Recipe courtesy of Chef Bennie Horne onboard the lugger Vanalburt-Lee *in 1967*
Yield: 6 servings

"We get the oysters around Chandeleur Island. You just jump overboard in your tennis shoes and pick up as many as you need."—Dr. A. C. Hewes, 1967

6 large artichokes
3 lemons, halved
Water to cover
Salt to taste
8 tablespoons unsalted butter
2 cups Mississippi oysters
1½ cups chopped onion
3 tablespoons all-purpose flour

½ cup beef broth
⅓ cup grated parmesan cheese
¼ cup lemon juice
1 bay leaf, crushed
½ teaspoon fresh thyme leaves
Pepper to taste
Tabasco or Crystal hot sauce to
    taste

Trim the stem off each artichoke and rub the ends of both the stem and the artichoke with the lemons. In a large pot, add enough water to cover the 6 artichokes, season the water with salt, and bring to a boil. Add the artichokes and stems, reduce the heat, and simmer until tender, about 30 minutes. Drain artichokes and set aside to cool.

After the artichokes have fully cooled, remove the exterior leaves and set aside. Clean the artichoke bottoms and reserve. Select 12 sturdy and perfect leaves from the ones removed to be used as garnish, and set aside. Using a spoon, scrape off the tender parts of the remaining leaves, which should produce about 1½ cups of scrapings. Add the stems.

In a medium saucepan, melt half the butter over low heat. Slowly add the oysters and cook for 3 to 4 minutes, or until the oysters start to curl. Do not overcook. Remove from the heat, strain the oysters, and set aside. Reserve the oyster liquor. Place the oysters in a food processor or blender, and on a low setting, lightly pulse 2 or 3 times until they are coarsely chopped. Set aside.

Heat the remaining butter in another saucepan over medium to low heat and add the onions. When the onions are nearly translucent, add the flour. Stir for about 5 minutes, then add the oyster liquor and artichoke scrapings. Stir.

Add the beef broth and reduce by about half. Add the parmesan, lemon juice, and bay leaf. Season with thyme, salt, pepper, and hot sauce. Simmer over low heat, stirring frequently, for about 30 minutes. Remove from the heat and after 5 minutes, add the chopped oysters. Stir well.

To serve, place an artichoke bottom on each plate and cover with the oyster and artichoke sauce. Arrange the reserved leaves on each plate for use as a scoop.

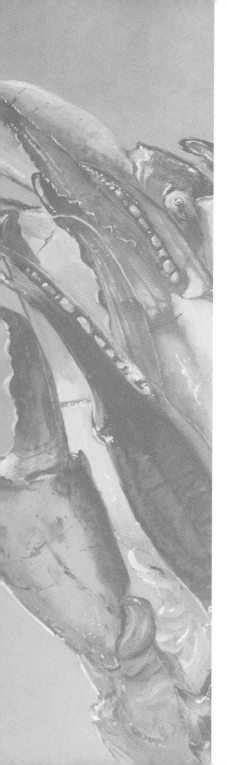

East Beach Minced Oysters

Recipe courtesy of Vivian Pringle Hewes
Yield: 12 to 15 servings

1 quart fresh Mississippi oysters
1 cup Italian breadcrumbs
8 tablespoons unsalted butter
1 large onion, minced
1 cup minced celery
1 bunch green onions, chopped
½ cup parsley, minced

Juice of 2 lemons
Splash of white wine
1 tablespoon Worcestershire sauce
2 teaspoons Crystal or Tabasco hot
   sauce
Salt and pepper to taste

Drain the oysters and reserve the oyster liquor. Using a clean pair of cooking shears or a knife, mince the oysters and set aside. Place the breadcrumbs in a separate bowl and pour in enough oyster liquor to make them moist and doughy.

In a skillet over medium heat, melt the butter and sauté the onions until they are translucent. Add the celery and sauté for 3 minutes. Turn heat to medium low, add the remaining ingredients except the oysters and breadcrumbs, and continue to cook.

Add the minced oysters and breadcrumbs and simmer for 1 minute longer. The consistency should be fairly thick, and the remaining oyster liquor can be used to adjust. Taste for seasoning.

Transfer to a serving bowl. Refrigerate for at least 1 hour or up to 1 day. Serve as a dip with fancy crackers.

Marinated Mississippi Blue Crabs

Recipe courtesy of Chef Bennie Horne onboard the lugger Vanalburt-Lee *in 1967*
Yield: 12 servings

Since 1944, members of the old coast Hewes family have been running an annual trip to Louisiana's Chandeleur Islands onboard their 46-foot lugger Vanalburt-Lee for two weeks of fishing. Chef Bennie Horne attended many of these trips and cooked what was described in a March 6, 1967, New York Times article as "some of the finest food of any vessel afloat on the Gulf Coast."

Water to cover
2 8-ounce bottles liquid crab boil
Salt to taste
3 dozen live Mississippi blue crabs
¼ cup lemon juice
¼ cup white-wine vinegar
1½ cups vegetable oil
1 cup minced celery
⅓ cup chopped bell pepper
⅓ cup capers
¾ cup pimento-stuffed green olives, chopped
¾ cup pitted black olives, chopped
3 cloves garlic, minced
½ teaspoon tarragon leaves
½ teaspoon chopped basil
¼ teaspoon thyme
¼ teaspoon oregano
Pepper to taste

In a large pot, add enough water to cover the crabs and bring to a rolling boil. Add the crab boil and salt to taste. Add the crabs to the pot and return to a boil. Then reduce the heat and let simmer for 15 minutes.

Remove from heat and let stand for another 5 minutes. Drain and let the crabs cool. Once the crabs are cool, rinse them in cool water. Then, using a large knife, split the crabs in half.

In a large mixing bowl, combine the remaining ingredients and mix well. Transfer the crabs to a very large resealable container and add the marinade. Toss to coat. Refrigerate for at least 2 to 3 days, turning the crab mixture regularly. Serve chilled or at a cool room temperature in a large bowl.

The next generation of the old-line Gulfport Hewes family takes the helm of their Biloxi lugger, which has been in the family since 1944.

Johnny Cakes with Jumbo Lump Blue Crab

Yield: 6 to 8 servings

Johnny Cakes
2 eggs
1 cup whole milk
¼ cup vegetable oil or bacon
   drippings
1½ cups Original Grit Girl cornmeal
1 cup all-purpose flour
2¼ teaspoons baking powder
¾ teaspoon kosher salt

Crabmeat Topping
8 tablespoons unsalted butter
1 large onion, medium diced

1 bunch green onions, coarsely
   chopped
4 cloves garlic, minced
Salt and pepper to taste
Dash of cayenne pepper
2 medium ripe Creole tomatoes,
   diced
6 slices bacon, cooked and crumbled
Splash of white wine
Juice of ½ lemon
1 pint Mississippi jumbo lump blue
   crabmeat, twice picked
Melted butter for basting

Johnny Cakes with Jumbo Lump Blue Crab.

For the johnny cakes, beat eggs in a mixing bowl. Stir in the milk and most of the oil (save some to grease the griddle). Add the cornmeal, flour, baking powder, and salt. Mix until smooth and pourable. If the batter is too thick, it can be thinned by adding a little more milk. For each johnny cake, pour about ¼ cup batter onto a hot, greased griddle. Each johnny cake should be no more than 2 to 3 inches wide. Lightly brown on both sides. Keep warm under a clean towel.

Heat a skillet over high heat, melt 6 tablespoons butter. Quickly add the onions, green onions, garlic, a little salt and pepper, and the dash of cayenne, while stirring rapidly. Add the tomatoes and cooked bacon and continue to stir. After 2 minutes, reduce the heat to low and deglaze the skillet with the wine and lemon juice. Add 2 tablespoons butter. Once melted, add the crabmeat. Cook for 2 minutes longer and then remove from the heat.

To serve, place 1 or 2 johnny cakes on each plate. Baste the top of each cake with melted butter before ladling a nice-sized scoop of the crab on top.

Grand Batture Hot Blue Crab Dip

Yield: 1 quart (party size)

This dish can be made ahead of time and refrigerated for 2 days. Gently reheat and then garnish before serving.

8 tablespoons butter
1 white onion, chopped
1 bell pepper, chopped
½ bunch green onions, chopped
3 stalks celery, chopped
6 cloves garlic, minced
½ teaspoon cayenne pepper
2 teaspoons Old Bay seasoning
Juice of 1 lemon
1 cup crumbled cooked apple-
smoked bacon

4 pounds cream cheese, cut into
chunks
1 pint heavy cream
½ pint half-and-half
2 pounds Mississippi jumbo lump
blue crabmeat, twice picked
1 tablespoon sherry
Salt and pepper to taste
Freshly grated parmesan cheese for
dusting
Green onions cut on a bias for garnish

In a large skillet, melt the butter over medium heat. Add the onions, bell pepper, green onions, and celery and cook until the vegetables are translucent and tender. Add the garlic, cayenne, and Old Bay seasoning and stir well. Add the lemon juice and crumbled bacon and stir.

Add the cream cheese, little by little, and let it melt. Then add the heavy cream and half-and-half. Stir well. When the mixture becomes thickened, fold in the crabmeat, sherry, salt, and pepper. Adjust seasonings as needed.

Transfer to a chafing dish to keep warm. Dust with cheese and garnish with green onions. Serve immediately and with fancy crackers.

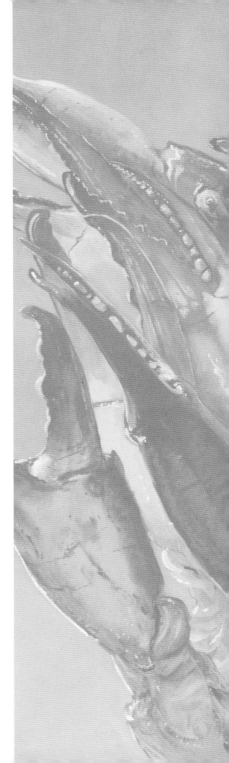

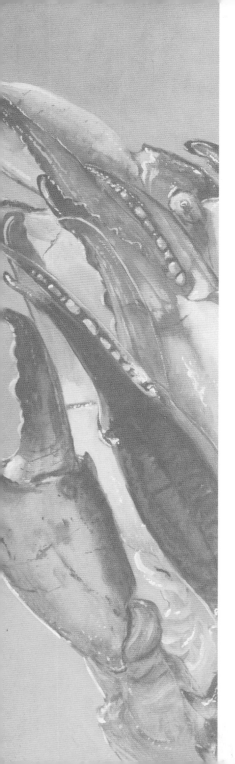

Biloxi Bacon

Yield: 6 to 8 servings

10 to 12 fresh mullet filets, skin
   removed
Salt and pepper to taste
1 cup all-purpose flour
2 eggs
½ cup half-and-half
¼ cup yellow mustard

1 box Zatarain's or other seasoned
   fish fry
1 cup bacon drippings
1 cup peanut oil
Comeback Sauce (see index)
Tartar Sauce (see index)

Season the mullet filets lightly with salt and pepper. Place the flour and a little salt and pepper in a shallow bowl. In another shallow bowl, whisk together the eggs, half-and-half, and yellow mustard. Place the seasoned fish fry in a third shallow bowl.

In a cast-iron skillet, heat the bacon drippings and oil over medium-high heat. Dredge the filets in the flour and shake off the excess. Dip filets in the egg wash, and then dredge in the fish fry.

Place in skillet and cook until they turn golden brown on one side, then turn the fish and continue to cook until they are golden brown on the second side, about 2 minutes per side. Transfer the fish to a paper-towel-lined plate to drain. Serve immediately with both Comeback Sauce and Tartar Sauce for dipping.

Rocks

Charbroiled "Rocks" with Andouille Sausage

Yield: 4 to 6 servings

1 pound butter
2 tablespoons minced garlic
1 tablespoon minced chives
1 tablespoon minced red onion
1 tablespoon cayenne pepper
1 tablespoon black pepper
1 tablespoon prepared horseradish

Juice of 1 lemon
4 dozen fresh Mississippi oysters,
 shucked and on the half-shell
¼ pound andouille sausage, grilled
 and small diced
1 pound parmesan cheese, grated

Heat a grill to medium high, about 400 degrees. In a saucepan over medium heat, melt the butter. Add the vegetables, spices, horseradish, and lemon juice and sauté for 3 to 4 minutes. Set aside and keep warm on the grill.

Place the shucked oysters on the half-shell on a baking sheet or a platter and then generously spoon the butter sauce onto each oyster. Place 1 teaspoon andouille sausage on top of each oyster, and then dust each oyster with the parmesan cheese. Cooking in batches, place 1 dozen oysters on the grill at a time. Close the lid and cook until the cheese is melted and turning golden brown and the oysters are beginning to curl around the edges, about 5 to 8 minutes.

Using tongs, carefully transfer the oysters to a serving tray. Repeat the process with the remaining oysters. Serve the oysters to your guests hot off the grill.

Rocks!

Charbroiled "Rocks" Rockefeller

Yield: 4 to 6 servings

15 ounces fresh spinach
8 ounces mustard or collard greens
1 bunch green onions
1 bunch parsley
6 ounces ketchup
4 ounces Worcestershire sauce
4 ounces Herbsaint
8 ounces anchovy paste
2 cloves garlic, peeled

Juice of ½ lemon
1 pound butter, melted
6 ounces Italian breadcrumbs
Salt, black pepper, and cayenne
   pepper to taste
4 dozen fresh Mississippi oysters,
   shucked and on the half-shell
3 cups freshly grated parmesan
   cheese

Wash the greens. Put all ingredients except for the oysters and parmesan into a food processor, and blend until the mixture is the consistency of soft-serve ice cream. More breadcrumbs may be added to tighten or more melted butter may be added to loosen the mixture as needed.

Heat a grill to medium high, about 400 degrees. Place the shucked oysters on the half-shell on a baking sheet or a platter and then generously spoon the "Rockefeller" sauce onto each oyster. Dust each oyster with the parmesan cheese. Cooking in batches, place 1 dozen oysters on the grill at a time. Close the lid and cook until the cheese is melted and turning golden brown and the oysters are beginning to curl around the edges, about 5 to 8 minutes.

Using tongs, carefully transfer the oysters to a serving tray. Repeat the process with the remaining oysters. Serve the oysters to your guests hot off the grill.

"Rocks" on the grill, drizzled with butter and green onions and always a heavy hand with the cayenne and other spices.

Charbroiled "Rocks" with Champagne Butter

Recipe courtesy of Brannon Janca, Stinky's Fish Camp
Yield: 4 to 6 servings

1 pound butter
¼ cup lemon juice
½ cup dry champagne
¼ cup parsley, chopped

Salt and black pepper to taste
4 dozen fresh Mississippi oysters,
   shucked and on the half-shell
4 cups grated gruyere cheese

Heat a grill to medium high, about 400 degrees. Place the butter in a food processor and pulse on low. When softened, pulse on high until whipped. Add the remaining ingredients except for the oysters and cheese. In a saucepan over medium heat. sauté the champagne butter for 3 to 4 minutes. Set aside and keep warm on the grill.

Place the shucked oysters on the half-shell on a baking sheet or a platter and then generously spoon the butter sauce onto each oyster. Place a pinch or two of the cheese on top of each oyster. Cooking in batches, place 1 dozen oysters on the grill at a time. Close the lid and cook until the cheese is melted and turning golden brown and the oysters are beginning to curl around the edges, about 5 to 8 minutes.

Using tongs, carefully transfer the oysters to a serving tray. Repeat the process with the remaining oysters. Serve the oysters to your guests hot off the grill.

Mignonette Dipping Sauce for Raw Oysters

Yield: 1½ cups

In coastal Mississippi, we tend to mask the natural flavor of our raw oysters with heavy and hot cocktail sauces. The mignonette sauce originates from France and accentuates the delicate taste of their coastal oysters. It works equally well with Mississippi oysters.

1 cup champagne vinegar
¼ cup red-wine vinegar
¼ cup rice-wine vinegar
1 teaspoon sugar
1 teaspoon fresh-ground white
   pepper

½ teaspoon red pepper flakes
1 teaspoon minced fresh ginger
¼ cup minced green onions

Combine all of the ingredients in a mixing bowl and whisk well. Cover and let sit in the refrigerator for 2 hours. To serve, drizzle the mignonette sauce onto raw oysters on the half-shell or place in a ramekin for dipping.

Reading the Wind

Like a great novel, sailors read the wind on the water. Wind lines are new chapters that guide them towards grand destinations, and approaching squalls are plot twists that must be surmounted to further their character arcs. William Faulkner and Eudora Welty both understood this as they sailed Mississippi's inland lakes or out to the barrier islands off the coast. Walter Anderson intertwined his life and art with these waters and sand-blown islands. Walker Percy wrote of daytrips from New Orleans to lounge on the beaches and enjoy the cooling breezes coming off the Mississippi Sound, desiring a boat with sails to capture them.

As far back as the early 1800s, wealthy bankers and cotton brokers from New Orleans understood the draw of the waters of the Mississippi Sound. In what would become an annual escape from the summer heat and yellow-fever epidemics of the city, they would sail their families over to the coast, where they kept second homes. Throughout the long summers they'd join their sailing counterparts from Pass Christian, Gulfport, and Biloxi and organize informal regattas that utilized the Gulf Islands as waypoints and sailing marks. Over two centuries later, nothing has changed.

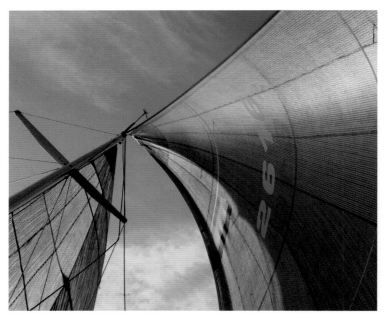

Sails full, sky above . . . everything is within reach.

Today marinas and yacht clubs from Bay St. Louis to Singing River, some over 150 years old, serve as outposts on the Mississippi Sound—beacons drawing sailors in from days spent on the water or pulling them down to the water's edge from points inland. Out on the piers, Olympic-class sailors easily mingle with novice adults and juniors learning this new way of life as the boat rigging clinks in the wind, waiting for hoisted sails.

As each new summer approaches, the ties to this deep history and its traditions breeze again onto the coast. In June, all ranges of sailors board boats in New Orleans and sail the nearly 175-year-old Race to the Coast, which culminates in Gulfport—the oldest point-to-point sailboat race in the Western Hemisphere. A week later, nearly 100 boats of every stripe will sail from Ship Island for Pensacola along the southern reaches of the Gulf barrier islands. These men and women are sharing an adventure, a sport that is akin to wilderness expeditions, and it creates enduring bonds and memories. For most sailors, the value is in the journey—the landfall is simply lagniappe. And many learn this as junior sailors, some as young as six, in sailing camps throughout the coast or on Jackson's Ross Barnett Reservoir.

Any local sailors under scholarship who aspire to the Olympics will tell you that they learned their skills sailing eight-foot Optimist dinghies at yacht clubs from Gulfport to Biloxi. In fact, most sailors will not hesitate to describe how they learned self-reliance out on the waters under the guidance of junior sailing programs.

The water and wind become a part of who these kids are, and the legacy gets passed down through generations. Three of the five oldest yacht clubs in the Americas are located on the Mississippi Coast, and family trees thread through their membership rolls.

Over the years, women have held a leadership role in the sport. Well before women had the right to vote in this country, all-female-crewed boats were openly competing against men, a disconcerting fact for their old-school male counterparts. There are several documented examples of all-female crews and regattas on the Gulf Coast dating back to 1904, and today female skippers, crew, and regattas are common, with one of the oldest sailed out of Pass Christian. Created by Commodore Bernard L. Knost, who was a major proponent of women's racing, the regatta that still bears his name morphed into an all-women's Gulf Yachting Association interclub championship held each summer.

While regattas are the most publicized events and certainly daunting for individuals with little to no sailing experience, racing constitutes a scant 15 percent of on-the-water activities. Cruising sailors, whether affiliated with a club or not, make up the vast majority of the sailing population. It is a liberating escape for families to set out on relaxed sails for the barrier islands and anchor in lee shores. Kids turn off their PlayStations to chase ghost crabs or simply run their feet through the sand, and adults put away their iPads to grill the day's catch off the sterns of sailboats over cocktails—these experiences create lasting memories.

With the Gulf Islands and their legacy of pirates and ancient forts within easy reach for daysailors, it's hard not to get wrapped up in the romanticism of sailing. And while aspects of this world my appear daunting to the uninitiated, most seasoned sailors are decked out in flip flops and readily accepting and willing to teach people who feel the call of the water. New families begin their legacies on the water every day, learning what it means to have that sail full in the breeze and those island shores within their grasp.

With many local fishermen being descendants of Yugoslavian immigrants, surnames ending in "ich" are incredibly common on the coast.

Salads

Soltario 06

Blue Crab Cakes Over Rocket

Yield: 4 to 6 servings

This dish is a celebration of the integrity of the blue crab.

Crab Cakes
1 red bell pepper
1 yellow bell pepper
1 green bell pepper
Olive oil
4 cloves garlic, peeled
2 eggs
1 tablespoon Duke's mayonnaise
1 teaspoon kosher salt
1 teaspoon black pepper
1 teaspoon Old Bay seasoning
1 teaspoon lemon juice
1 pound fresh Mississippi lump blue
   crabmeat, twice picked
1 cup crushed saltines
2 tablespoons diced red onion

Lemon Vinaigrette
6 tablespoons Steen's cane vinegar
2 tablespoons lemon juice
2 teaspoons Creole mustard
1 teaspoon kosher salt
1 teaspoon black pepper
1 teaspoon unrefined brown cane
   sugar
½ cup extra-virgin olive oil

Salad
5 ounces rocket (arugula)
½ red onion, thinly sliced
6 crab cakes
1 cup grape tomatoes, halved
Lemon Vinaigrette

Rub the peppers with oil and place them directly on the open flame of a gas stove. Rotate occasionally as the peppers begin to char and blister. Let the peppers char on all sides. Place the peppers in a paper bag or a glass bowl covered with plastic wrap. Once they are cool, remove and discard the stems, skins, and seeds, and dice the peppers. Reserve 3 tablespoons of each pepper for the crab cakes and reserve the rest for later use. They can be frozen for up to 1 month.

Preheat the oven to 350 degrees. Place the garlic cloves on a square of foil, drizzle them with 1 teaspoon olive oil, and close the package. Bake for 20 minutes. Remove from the oven and mince.

In a mixing bowl, whisk together the eggs, mayonnaise, garlic, salt, pepper, and Old Bay seasoning. Fold the remaining ingredients into the mixture. Scoop enough of the mixture to make a 3-inch-wide patty, about ½ cup. Repeat with the remaining mixture. Refrigerate the crab cakes until firm, at least 30 minutes.

Add 2 teaspoons olive oil to a cast-iron skillet over medium heat and sauté the crab cakes until they become a light golden brown on each side, 2 to 3 minutes. Transfer to a platter and place in a warm oven.

For the vinaigrette, in a medium-size mixing bowl, combine all of the ingredients except for the olive oil, and whisk together. Slowly drizzle the olive oil into the bowl while continuously whisking. Whisk until well incorporated. Set aside.

To assemble, arrange a bed of rocket and red onion slices on each plate. Place a single crab cake in the center, garnish with the grape tomatoes, drizzle with the freshly shaken vinaigrette, and serve.

Crabmeat Lizette with Bloody Mary Aspic

Recipe courtesy of Stacey Meyer
Yield: 4 servings

Bloody Mary Aspic
3 tablespoons powdered gelatin,
    about 4½ packs of Knox
¼ cup cool water
3 cups your favorite Bloody Mary mix
¼ cup vodka
1 tablespoon lemon juice
2 teaspoons hot sauce
1 teaspoon Worcestershire sauce
¾ teaspoon salt
¼ teaspoon black pepper

Crabmeat Lizette
¾ cup homemade or store-bought
    mayonnaise

2 tablespoons chopped fresh chives,
    plus 1 tablespoon for garnish
1 tablespoon Dijon mustard
1 tablespoon chopped fresh chervil
1 tablespoon chopped fresh basil
1 tablespoon freshly squeezed
    lemon juice
½ teaspoon hot sauce
½ teaspoon salt
¼ teaspoon freshly ground white
    pepper
1 pound fresh Mississippi lump blue
    crabmeat, twice picked
2 ripe avocados
2 tablespoons lime juice

To make the aspic, in a small bowl or measuring cup, sprinkle the gelatin over the water and let the gelatin bloom for 2 to 3 minutes. Heat the gelatin mixture in the microwave just until the gelatin begins to dissolve, about 10 seconds. Stir well. Pour the gelatin into the Bloody Mary mix and stir until blended. Stir in the vodka, lemon juice, hot sauce, Worcestershire, salt, and pepper. The aspic will begin to set up, so work quickly. Carefully pour the mixture into an 8-inch oiled baking dish and transfer it to the refrigerator. Let the aspic set up for at least 2 hours.

In a medium-size mixing bowl, combine the mayonnaise, chives, mustard, chervil, basil, lemon juice, hot sauce, ¼ teaspoon salt, and pepper, and mix well. Gently fold in the crabmeat. Refrigerate, covered, until ready to use.

Peel and remove the pits from the avocados, and cut the avocados into ¼-inch chunks. In a small bowl, toss the avocados with the lime juice and remaining salt.

To serve, cut the aspic into 3-inch rounds using a ring mold or round cookie cutter. Gently transfer each round to a plate. Scoop ¼ of the avocado into the ring mold and press down lightly. Place ¼ of the crabmeat on top and press down into the mold. Set the ring mold over an aspic round and carefully remove the ring mold. Garnish with the chives. Repeat with the remaining 3 servings.

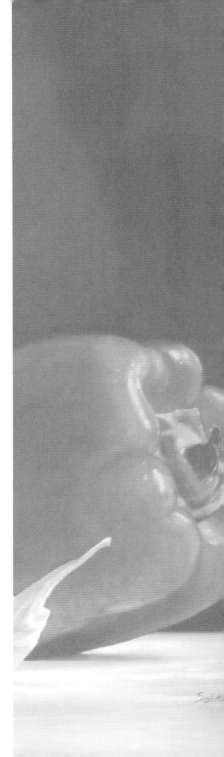

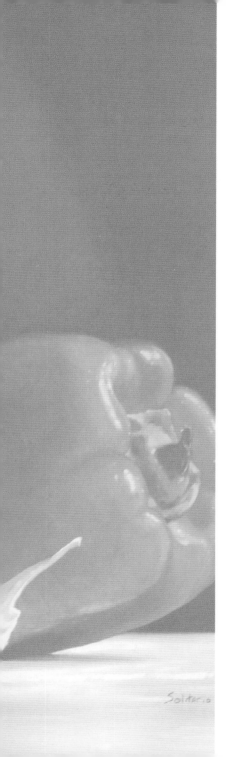

Crabmeat Jubilee

Yield: 6 to 8 servings

1 cup homemade or store-bought
  mayonnaise
¼ cup chili sauce
2 tablespoons chopped green
  onions
2 tablespoons chopped parsley
Juice of 1 lemon
1 teaspoon prepared horseradish

1 teaspoon Worcestershire sauce
2 or 3 splashes Bonney's or Crystal
  Hot Sauce
Salt and black pepper to taste
1 pound fresh Mississippi lump blue
  crabmeat, twice picked
2 large Creole tomatoes, diced
1 head iceberg lettuce, shredded

In a large salad bowl, combine the mayonnaise, chili sauce, green onions, parsley, lemon juice, horseradish, Worcestershire, hot sauce, and salt and pepper, and mix well. Fold in the crabmeat carefully so as not to break up the large pieces. Add the tomatoes and lettuce to the crabmeat mixture and toss gently. Serve.

West Indies Salad

Yield: 4 to 6 servings

Dressing
½ cup lemon juice
½ cup extra-virgin olive oil
4 teaspoons white-wine vinegar
Pinch of cayenne pepper
1 teaspoon kosher salt
½ teaspoon dry mustard
1 teaspoon black pepper
1 teaspoon red pepper flakes

Salad
10 ounces Romaine lettuce
2-3 avocados, cut into wedges
2 large Creole tomatoes, cut into ½-
    inch wedges
1 large red onion, thinly sliced
1 pound fresh Mississippi lump blue
    crabmeat, twice picked

In a small bowl, combine all of the dressing ingredients. Whisk well and set aside.

Arrange a bed of the lettuce on each plate. Uniformly arrange the wedges of avocado and Creole tomato and interspace with the red onion slices. Place 1 tablespoon crabmeat in the center, drizzle with the freshly shaken vinaigrette, and serve.

Pickled Shrimp in a Celery and Fennel Salad

Recipe courtesy of Alex Perry, Vestige Restaurant, Ocean Springs
Yield: 6 servings

Pickled Shrimp (see index)

Rouille Sauce
1 large red bell pepper
1 large clove garlic
¼ cup red-wine vinegar
1 egg
½ teaspoon smoked paprika
½ teaspoon sugar
¾ teaspoon kosher salt
2 cups canola oil or other light-
    tasting oil
1/16 teaspoon xanthan gum

Dill Oil
3 packed cups fresh dill
1 cup canola oil

Poached Potato
1 Yukon gold potato
2 teaspoons extra-virgin olive oil
½ teaspoon salt

Celery and Fennel Salad
2 stalks celery
1 fennel bulb
1 teaspoon extra-virgin olive oil
Maldon salt
3 celery leaves
5 small fennel fronds

For the rouille, roast the bell pepper on the open flame of a gas stove until heavily charred. Place the pepper in a stainless-steel bowl, cover tightly with plastic wrap, and allow to steam for 15 minutes. Gently peel off the charred skin, and remove the stem and seeds from inside while reserving any juice from inside the pepper. Roughly chop the pepper and garlic clove. In a blender, add the chopped pepper and garlic, reserved pepper juice, vinegar, egg, paprika, sugar, and salt. Blend on high until the mixture is smooth. On low speed, slowly drizzle in the canola oil. Once oil is incorporated, add the xanthan gum and briefly blend on medium speed. The rouille can be made up to 2 days in advance and stored in an airtight container in the refrigerator.

For the dill oil, blanch the dill in boiling water for 15 seconds. Transfer dill to an ice bath and chill for 10 minutes. Squeeze out excess moisture and place the dill in a blender. Blend with the canola oil on high speed for 30 seconds. Allow oil to infuse overnight, then strain through a fine-mesh strainer into another container.

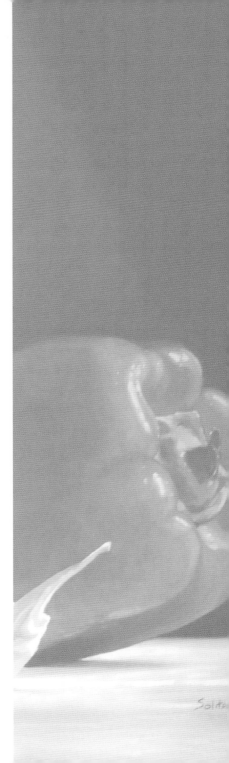

The dill oil will last for about 3 days in the refrigerator in a resealable container.

For the poached potato, slice the potato on a mandoline ⅛ inch thick. Using a small ring cutter, cut out circles from each of the potato slices. Cook potatoes in a pot of boiling, salted water until tender, about 8 minutes. Season with oil and salt and set aside.

For the salad, using a sharp peeler, peel off long, thin ribbons of celery. Split the fennel in half lengthwise. Remove the outer layer. Slice each half of fennel crosswise very thinly until you reach the core. Blanch the celery and fennel in a pot of boiling salted water for 10 seconds. Place celery and fennel in an ice bath and chill for 10 minutes. Remove from ice and dry them on paper towels.

To assemble, cut the shrimp in to large chunks and dry on a paper towel. Spoon some of the rouille sauce into the center of a chilled serving bowl, and spoon dill oil around the sauce. Arrange the potato circles and shrimp over the sauce. Coat the celery and fennel in the olive oil, sprinkle with Maldon salt, and place around the potatoes and shrimp. Place the celery leaves and fennel fronds over the dish. Sprinkle Maldon salt over the finished dish.

Sunset over Deer Island, with the shrimpers heading south into the Sound. Many will spend days offshore until their holds are full.

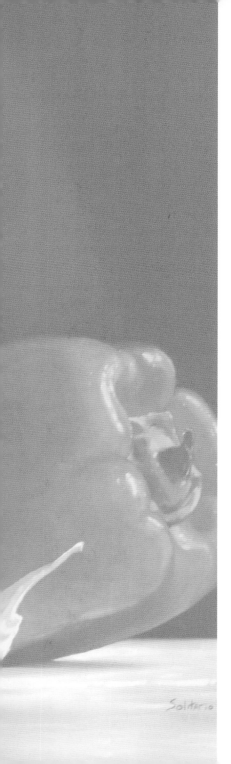

Fried Crawfish with Rocket and a Tangerine-Honey Vinaigrette

Yield: 4 to 6 servings

Tangerine-Honey Vinaigrette
1 teaspoon minced red onion
¼ cup rice-wine vinegar
1 teaspoon Creole mustard
1 teaspoon honey
1 teaspoon Sriracha
1 teaspoon freshly squeezed lime juice
2 tablespoons freshly squeezed tangerine juice
6 tablespoons extra-virgin olive oil
¼ teaspoon kosher salt
¼ teaspoon fresh-ground black pepper

Fried Crawfish with Rocket
1 cup all-purpose flour
2 eggs
½ cup half-and-half
1 box Zatarain's or other seasoned fish fry
2 tablespoons extra-virgin olive oil
1 pound peeled crawfish tails
10 ounces rocket, cut in a chiffonade
¼ cup minced red onion
¼ cup thinly sliced radish
1 cup crumbled feta cheese

Place all the vinaigrette ingredients in a small mixing bowl and whisk well. Set aside.

Place the flour in a shallow bowl. In another shallow bowl, whisk together the eggs and half-and-half. Place the fish fry in a third shallow bowl.

In a skillet over medium-high heat, add the olive oil. Dredge the crawfish in the flour and shake off the excess. Then dip into the egg wash and dredge in the fish fry. Fry the crawfish in batches until they turn golden brown. Drain on a paper-towel-lined plate.

Arrange a bed of rocket , red onion, and radish slices on each plate. Place a handful of fried crawfish in the center, garnish with the feta cheese, drizzle with the freshly shaken vinaigrette, and serve.

ON THE COAST

Cracklin Cobb Salad

Yield: 6 to 8 servings

1 tablespoon butter
¼ pound raw pork cracklins, diced
½ pound Romaine lettuce
½ pound iceberg lettuce
4 eggs, hardboiled and chopped
½ pound apple-smoked bacon,
   cooked and chopped
2 pickled beets, thinly sliced

2 carrots, peeled and julienned
1 radish, julienned
1 cucumber, thinly sliced
1 cup shredded Mississippi State
   University cheddar cheese
1 medium red onion, thinly sliced
1 cup Comeback Sauce (see index)
2 slices cornbread

In a cast-iron skillet, melt the butter over medium heat and fry the cracklins until golden brown. In a large salad bowl, add all of the ingredients except for the cornbread and toss thoroughly. To serve, divide the salad among 6 to 8 plates and crumble the cornbread on top.

Government Street Grocery's Cole Slaw

Recipe courtesy of Patrick Sullivan, Government Street Grocery, Ocean Springs
Yield: 10 servings (party size)

Be sure to fully chill the dressing before pouring it over the vegetables, to avoid wilting the slaw!

Dressing
1½ cups sugar
2 teaspoons dry mustard
2 teaspoons celery seed
2 tablespoons salt
2 cups apple-cider vinegar
1 cup vegetable oil
4 tablespoons honey

Cole Slaw
2 heads cabbage, shredded
2 red bell peppers, chopped
3 green bell peppers, chopped
1 large red onion, chopped
2 heads celery, chopped
1½ cups julienned or shredded
  carrots

Place all of the dressing ingredients in a small pot. Bring almost to a boil while stirring. Immediately remove from heat. Allow to cool, then place in a container and chill in the refrigerator.

Place the vegetables in a large mixing bowl. When the dressing is fully chilled, pour over the vegetables and mix well with a large spoon. Transfer to a large container and refrigerate for at least 1 hour before serving.

Government Street Grocery is the vanguard of live music and great local food in Ocean Springs.

Ms. Betty's Congealed Cranberry Salad

Recipe courtesy of Ms. Elizabeth Julia "Betty" Werling Snider Oliver
Yield: 8 to 10 servings

It's obvious from old Mississippi Coast cookbooks, especially ones from the 1950s, '60s, and '70s, that Mississippi loved congealed salads back then. It is therefore highly appropriate to reach out to the past and include here a tasty gelatin-based treat. This recipe is from a dear friend's mother who was born in Port Gibson in 1927 and was married in 1949 in Bay St. Louis. She resided in Old Jefferson, just outside of New Orleans, until she passed away in 2011.

1 small can pineapple slices,
   drained and juice reserved
1 can mandarin orange segments,
   drained and juice reserved
1½ cups water or cranberry juice
2 3-ounce packages cherry Jell-O or
   Royal gelatin

1 16-ounce can Ocean Spray
   cranberry sauce
½ cup minced celery
½ cup pecans, chopped

In a pot, combine the reserved fruit juices. Add enough water or cranberry juice to make 1½ cups of liquid total. Bring to a boil and pour over the gelatin in a mixing bowl. Stir until the gelatin is completely dissolved. Add the cranberry sauce and whisk until the cranberry sauce has melted. Allow mixture to cool, then transfer to the refrigerator to set up. Once the gelatin has begun to firm up, add the fruit, celery, and pecans to the mixture. Ladle the mixture into a mold and cover with plastic wrap. Return to the refrigerator and allow to cool for a minimum of 8 hours. To unmold, invert over the serving dish and apply a hot, dampened towel over the exterior of the mold. Serve with greens and fruit around the cranberry salad.

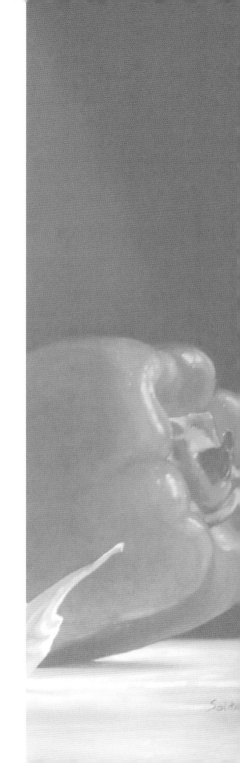

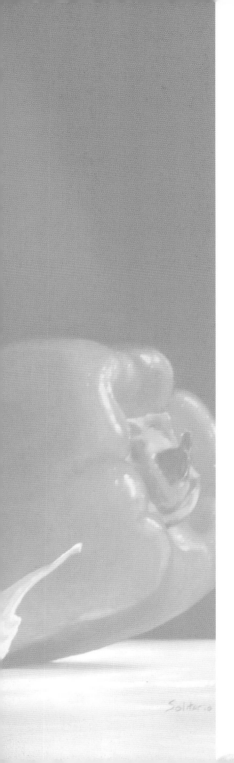

Wolf River Egg Salad

Yield: 8 to 10 servings

To lessen the heat in this spicy dish, simply reduce the amount of Sriracha to your taste.

10 hardboiled eggs, peeled with yolks and whites separated
1 tablespoon Sriracha
1 pint homemade or store-bought mayonnaise
¾ pound bacon, cooked and crumbled

1 small red bell pepper, minced
1 small red onion, minced
1 tablespoon fresh-ground black pepper
1 teaspoon Tony Chachere's Creole Seasoning

In a large mixing bowl, combine the hardboiled yolks with the Sriracha and mayonnaise and mix well. Add the remaining ingredients except for the egg whites and mix thoroughly. Chop the egg whites and fold them in.

Serve slathered onto your favorite sandwich bread or refrigerate for use later.

Who wouldn't be as cool as this skipper while helming a Biloxi lugger? (Photograph courtesy of the Pass Christian Yacht Club)

Pickling

Pickling Liquor

Yield: About 4 pints

Local farmers' markets are filled with harvests from the coast and the interior of the state, and Mississippians have a storied tradition of pickling fresh vegetables for snacks or to use as garnish for Bloody Marys during college football season. Fresh okra, snap beans, peppers, carrots, radishes, and even beets make for ideal pickling items.

Pickling vegetables of your choice	6 cloves garlic, coarsely chopped
1 red onion, coarsely chopped	1 tablespoon coarsely chopped
2 jalapeno peppers, julienned	fresh ginger
4 bay leaves	1 tablespoon red pepper flakes
2 cups apple-cider vinegar	1 tablespoon celery seed
1 cup water	1 tablespoon whole cloves
1½ cups sugar	1 tablespoon ground cloves
1 tablespoon fine salt	1 tablespoon mustard seeds

Sterilize 4 pint-size Mason jars.

Chefs Note: Spiciness can be adjusted by adding more or less of the red pepper flakes. You may also reduce the sweetness by using less sugar. Boiled and shelled eggs are an excellent item for pickling and an old-school Mississippi treat.

Pickling vegetables or seafood such as shrimp is very straightforward if they are to be consumed within a few days after refrigeration. However, for longer-term storage, please consult books or other guides specifically dedicated to long-term food preservation.

Slice or julienne the pickling vegetables and stuff into the Mason jars along with 1 tablespoon red onion, 1 or 2 slivers jalapeno, and 1 bay leaf per container. Set aside.

In a large pot over medium to high heat, simmer the remaining pickling ingredients until the salt and sugar are dissolved. Fill each jar completely with the hot pickling liquor, ensuring that plenty of garlic and ginger get into each container. Seal tightly, rinse, and dry each jar.

Mark the pickling date on the lid of each container, then place in the refrigerator. Marinate the vegetables at least 24 hours, periodically agitating each container. Enjoy.

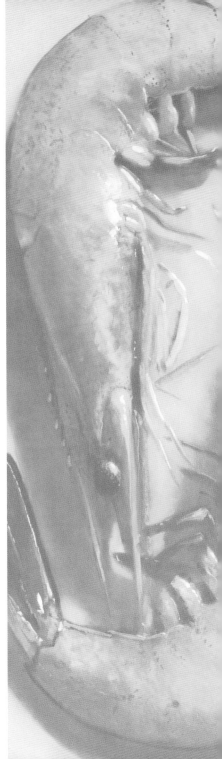

From fresh shrimp to nearly every vegetable imaginable, pickling adds a whole other flavor and dimension to storing and utilizing the state's bounty.

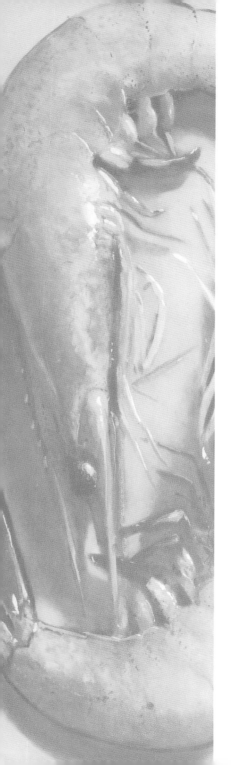

Pickled Shrimp

Recipe courtesy of Alex Perry, Vestige Restaurant, Ocean Springs
Yield: About 4 pints

The bounty of the Mississippi Sound can also be pickled and stored for later use and makes for an unrivaled late-night snack while anchored off of Horn Island.

1½ cups apple-cider vinegar
½ cup lemon juice
½ cup orange juice
¼ cup lime juice
¼ cup extra-virgin olive oil
1 clove garlic, smashed
2 teaspoons mustard seeds
2 teaspoons coriander seeds

1 teaspoon red pepper flakes
3 juniper berries
2 bay leaves
1 tablespoon kosher salt
1 pound jumbo (U16/20) fresh
   Mississippi white shrimp, peeled
   and deveined

Combine all ingredients except for the shrimp in a nonreactive saucepot. Bring to a simmer over medium heat, and cook gently for 2 minutes. Remove from heat, add the shrimp, and let stand for 12 to 15 minutes or until the shrimp are cooked. Transfer the shrimp and the liquid to a nonreactive container and refrigerate overnight. The shrimp can be stored in the refrigerator in a resealable container for 2 weeks.

Chef's Note: Pickling vegetables or seafood such as shrimp is very straightforward if they are to be consumed within a few days after refrigeration. However, for longer-term storage, please consult books or other guides specifically dedicated to long-term food preservation.

Gulf Island Restoration

The barrier islands of Mississippi help to form natural bays and protect estuaries that are crucial to sustaining some of the most productive recreational and commercial fisheries in North America. They also act as an important first line of hurricane defense for the Mississippi Gulf Coast. Often bearing the full force of these storms, these islands have been subjected to extreme weather events throughout their estimated 4,500-year history. These sandy, narrow, mostly undeveloped spits of land paralleling the coast act as speed bumps for storm surge and protect the populated coastline and infrastructure, but they also protect the breeding grounds and nurseries for the life cycle of fisheries. For centuries, natural processes replenished and repaired storm damage to these islands, but since the 1960s, giant swaths have been carved out of some and erosion is now systemic, with loss rates dramatically accelerating in the last few decades due to human activity.

Hurricane Betsy in 1965 and then Camille in 1969 pounded the Mississippi Coast. Through massive erosion and overwash, they split Ship Island in half and created what is now known as the Camille Cut, as well as East and West Ship islands. Hurricane Katrina enlarged the Camille Cut and also reopened a wide pass into the western side of Alabama's Dauphin Island in 2005. This cut into Dauphin Island occurred during several other major storms—Petit Bois Island originally broke off of Dauphin Island in the 18th century, but naturally. While federally protected to varying degrees since 1971, the issue hasn't been development pressures on the barrier islands located in the Gulf Islands National Seashore, but the dredging and deepening of shipping channels from the relatively shallow nearshore waters into the deep waters of the Gulf of Mexico.

With the prevailing current and winds, sands have historically and naturally eroded from the eastern islands and migrated to the west, up to 130 feet a year. This process tends to create shoaling and even periodic islands appearing where before there were none. In 1917, a small island emerged between Horn and Ship islands off the Mississippi Coast that would be developed into a resort and casino during Prohibition. Due to natural erosion patterns, by 1932, the Isle of Capri and all developments had washed away.

With the dredging of these channels to increasingly greater

The natural beauty found on Mississippi's federally protected coastal islands rivals that of any barrier island on the Gulf Coast. Located a quick 7 to 10 miles offshore, these islands are undeveloped and pristine, although eroding and at real risk of being lost.

depths to accommodate modern shipping, the natural repair mechanisms have failed. The replenishing sand in the water column is grabbed by these channels, which act as sand sinks and have contributed to the dramatically increased speed of erosion. According to the United States Geological Survey, Petit Bois Island has shrunk by 50 percent and Ship Island has lost nearly 65 percent of its landmass since 1917. The losses have accelerated in direct proportion to the widening and deepening of these channels throughout the Gulf Coast.

While the growing frequency of intense hurricanes and the normal issue of cold fronts stirring up the shallow waters and bays off the coast contribute to the erosion and narrowing of these islands, sometimes dramatically, the one manageable issue is the need for proper placement of beach-quality dredge back into the water-transport system or directly onto the islands themselves.

Sand removed from dredging has been placed on Ship Island periodically, to protect the historic Fort Massachusetts. In 2009, the U.S. Army Corps of Engineers proposed a nearly $500 million plan to re-nourish Petit Bois and Horn and close the three-plus-mile-wide Camille Cut in Ship Island. The first phase of this work was completed in 2011 with the reconstruction of nearly 300 feet of the northern beaches of West Ship Island, and the second phase, which includes the massive project of closing the Camille Cut, is expected to begin in the next few years.

Understanding the importance of these barrier islands as speed bumps during hurricanes and as contributing to natural fisheries, Dan Brown, park superintendent for the Gulf Islands National Seashore, states, "For decades, we had a limited understanding of barrier island systems. It wasn't until researchers started documenting and correlating the deepening of these channels to their land loss that we began to understand what was happening."

These barrier islands throughout the Northern Gulf Coast are important ecosystems and breeding grounds for seabirds and turtles as well as the incredibly bountiful shrimp and oyster harvesting waters. Couple these important issues with the natural protections against storm surge for the developed coastlines, and there is a real intersection of development, recreational/commercial fishing, and preservation interests that should be occurring all along the coast. Neglected for far too long, these investments are a first step in restoring the islands and will continue to give sportsmen ample opportunities to reel in those red snappers and speckled trout, while nearby the surf rolls on the quiet sugar-sand beaches and dunes of the Mississippi Gulf Coast.

Soups, Bisques, and Gumbos

"Leftover Shrimp Boil" Shrimp and Corn Chowder

Yield: 6 to 8 servings

This recipe explains how to prepare the dish from scratch, but leftover shrimp, corn, and potatoes from a shrimp boil the day before may be substituted. Peeled crawfish and the corn and potatoes from a crawfish boil will also work!

4 quarts water
1 8-ounce bottle liquid crab boil
2 pounds jumbo (U16/20) fresh
   Mississippi shrimp
2 pints heavy cream
1 pint whole milk
3 tablespoons butter

1 large onion, diced
1 green bell pepper, diced
1 teaspoon Old Bay seasoning
2 ears fresh corn
3 new potatoes, chopped
3 green onions, coarsely chopped

Bring the water to a boil in a large pot and add the liquid crab boil. Add the shrimp and remove from heat. Let stand for 5 minutes, strain the shrimp carefully, and set aside to cool. Once cool, peel the shrimp, coarsely chop, and set aside.

Pour the heavy cream and milk into a saucepot. Bring the mixture to a low simmer, being careful not to scald it. Reduce it by ⅓ and set aside on low heat.

Melt the butter in a large pot over medium-low heat. Add the onions, green peppers, and Old Bay seasoning. Cook, stirring frequently, until the onions are nearly caramelized, about 5 minutes. While this is cooking, take a heavy-duty knife and shave the corn kernels from the cobs. Add the potatoes and corn kernels to the pot, and continue to cook until the corn and potatoes also begin to caramelize. Once this happens, slowly pour the heavy cream and milk mixture into the pot. Mix thoroughly and simmer on medium heat until the cream is reduced by half. Add the chopped shrimp and allow to simmer for 2 to 3 minutes. Check seasoning and adjust as necessary. Serve with the green onions as garnish.

Singing River Shrimp Stew

Yield: 10 to 12 servings

8 tablespoons butter, melted
1 cup all-purpose flour
3 large onions, chopped
1 bunch green onions, chopped
4 stalks celery, chopped
4 cloves garlic, minced
Salt and black pepper to taste
4 teaspoons cayenne pepper
3 bay leaves, crushed
2 teaspoons thyme

4 ripe tomatoes, chopped
9 cups water
4 teaspoons freshly squeezed lemon
  juice
5 pounds white potatoes, peeled
  and sliced into rounds
5 pounds jumbo (U16/20) fresh
  Mississippi shrimp, peeled and
  deveined

In a large pot over medium heat, melt the butter. When it bubbles, add the flour and cook, stirring constantly, until you have a dark-chocolate roux. Reduce the heat to medium low and add the onions and celery. Cook until the onions are nearly translucent. Deglaze with ¼ cups of water as needed. Add the garlic, salt, pepper, and cayenne and stir thoroughly. Add the bay leaves and thyme, and stir well. Cook for 3 minutes longer. Add the tomatoes, water, and lemon juice and return to a low simmer. Simmer, covered, for 1 hour, stirring often. Add the potatoes, cover, and simmer for 15 minutes longer. Add the shrimp, reduce the heat, stir, cover, and cook for another 25 minutes. Serve in bowls with crusty French bread for dipping.

Square Handkerchief Oyster Stew

Yield: 6 to 8 servings

2 tablespoons butter	½ teaspoon Cajun seasoning
1 onion, diced	Pinch of nutmeg
3 cloves garlic, minced	1 pint fresh Mississippi oysters
½ cup minced fennel	1 bunch green onions, chopped
Oyster liquor	Pinch of cayenne pepper
1 pint heavy cream	Pernod or Ricard to drizzle
1 pint half-and-half	

In a large pot over medium heat, melt the butter. Add the onions, garlic, and fennel, and sweat until the onions are translucent, about 5 minutes. Deglaze with ¼ cup of the oyster liquor reserved from the pint of oysters, and stir. Reduce the heat to medium low and add the heavy cream, half-and-half, Cajun seasoning, and nutmeg. Lower the heat, bring to a simmer, and reduce the liquid by ⅓, about 10 minutes. Add the oysters and all of the remaining oyster liquor and stir. When the edges of the oysters begin to curl, prepare to serve. Ladle the stew into bowls or mugs, and garnish each with a sprinkle of green onions and a dusting of cayenne pepper. Finish each with ½ teaspoon Pernod or Ricard drizzled on top.

(Photograph courtesy of the United States Coast Guard)

Oyster Rockefeller Soup

Recipe courtesy of Edward Thornton, Tiki, Pascagoula
Yield: 6 to 8 servings

10 tablespoons unsalted butter
1 cup diced onions
1½ cups chopped raw bacon
5 cups fresh spinach, chopped
1½ teaspoons minced garlic
1 teaspoon kosher salt
1 teaspoon Creole seasoning
1½ pints fresh Mississippi oysters
1 tablespoon Louisiana Hot Sauce
1 tablespoon Worcestershire sauce

8 cups heavy cream
4 tablespoons freshly grated
  parmesan cheese
2 eggs
½ cup half-and-half
1 cup all-purpose flour
1 box Zatarain's or other seasoned
  fish fry
2 tablespoons extra-virgin olive oil

In a large skillet, melt 2 tablespoons butter over medium heat. Add the onions. When the onions become soft and translucent, about 5 minutes, add the bacon and sauté until crisp. Add the fresh spinach and cook until tender. Add the garlic, salt, and Creole seasoning. Transfer the mixture to a large soup pot. Reserving 8 to 10 oysters, add the remaining oysters and the oyster liquor to the pot and simmer on low heat for 8 minutes. Add the hot sauce, Worcestershire, and heavy cream, and return to a low simmer. Add the parmesan cheese.

Place the flour in a shallow bowl. In another shallow bowl, whisk together the eggs and half-and-half. Place the fish fry in a third shallow bowl.

In a skillet over medium-high heat, add the olive oil and melt the remaining butter. Dredge the oysters in the flour and shake off the excess. Then dip into the egg wash and dredge in the fish fry. Place in the skillet and cook until they turn golden brown on all sides. When the cheese is fully melted in the soup, serve garnished with a fried oyster or two.

Sycamore House Sunchoke Soup

Recipe courtesy of Stella LaGardeur, Sycamore House, Bay St. Louis
Yields: 6 servings

1¼ pounds Jerusalem artichokes
½ stalk lemongrass
1 tablespoon unsalted butter
½ medium yellow onion, diced
2 cups water

14 ounces heavy cream
Salt and white pepper to taste
Sour cream or crème fraiche for
  garnish

Peel and slice Jerusalem artichokes. Place in a bowl of water until ready to use. Remove the outer leaves of the lemongrass and split the stalk lengthwise. Bruise the fibers using the back of a chef's knife or a tenderizing mallet.

In a large heavy-gauge Dutch oven over medium-high heat, melt the butter. Add the onions and, stirring frequently, simmer them until translucent, about 10 minutes. Drain the Jerusalem artichokes from the water and then add them to the pot. Reduce the heat to medium. Cook stirring frequently, until they start to release their juices, about 10 minutes.

Add the water and lemongrass, and simmer until reduced by half. Reduce the heat to medium low and stir in the cream. Gently simmer the soup until the sunchokes are soft, about 30 to 40 minutes. Remove from heat.

Remove lemongrass from the pot and discard. Working in small batches, puree the soup until smooth and then pass through a fine-mesh strainer. Season with salt and pepper to taste. Serve the soup hot, garnished with the sour cream or crème fraiche.

Candied Sweet Potato Bisque with Italian Sausage

Yield: 12 servings

1 to 2 pounds hot Italian sausage
3 tablespoons olive oil
3 large onions, chopped
2 medium green bell peppers, chopped
3 carrots, peeled and chopped
3 stalks celery, chopped
4 green onions, sliced, with white and green separated
2 teaspoons chili powder
¼ teaspoon cayenne pepper
1 tablespoon Chinese 5 spice powder

7 large sweet potatoes, peeled and sliced about ½ inch thick
2 cups sherry
2 tablespoons minced garlic
6 quarts chicken stock
2 cups freshly squeezed orange juice
2 tablespoons Worcestershire sauce
3 tablespoons soy sauce
2 cups heavy cream
Salt and black pepper to taste

Roast the Italian sausage in the oven until cooked, about 6 to 8 minutes. Transfer to a paper-towel-lined plate. When cool, slice and set aside. In a large skillet over medium heat, add the oil. When hot, cook the onions, bell peppers, and carrots until the onions just begin to caramelize. Add the celery and green onions (white parts) and stir. Add the dry spices and sauté together until you can smell the spices rising from the pan, about 1 minute. Add the sweet potatoes and deglaze the pan with the sherry. Sauté briefly before transferring to a large saucepot, then add the garlic, stock, orange juice, Worcestershire, and soy. Simmer over medium-low heat for 1½ hours until the ingredients soften. Remove from heat and cool slightly. Puree in a blender, several batches at a time, until smooth. Return the bisque to the pot and add the sausage. Bring back up to a simmer and cook for 5 minutes longer. Add the heavy cream and salt and pepper to taste. Serve with green onion tops as garnish.

Corn and Crab Bisque

Yield: 6 to 8 servings

Crab Stock
1½ quarts water
2 large onions, coarsely chopped
6 stalks celery, coarsely chopped
2 tablespoons liquid crab boil
½ cup sugar
1 tablespoon kosher salt
5 live Mississippi blue crabs, rinsed

Bisque
8 tablespoons butter
1½ cups chopped green onions,
    green only
2 tablespoons all-purpose flour
1 teaspoon thyme
3 cloves garlic, minced
2 12-ounce cans corn kernels,
    drained
1½ cups heavy cream
2 pounds fresh Mississippi lump
    blue crabmeat, twice picked
¼ cup fresh parsley, chopped
Dash of liquid crab boil
Cajun seasoning to taste
Salt and black pepper to taste

Place all of the stock ingredients except for the crabs in a large pot and bring to a boil. Once boiling, add the crabs. Cover and simmer for 30 minutes. Remove from heat and let stand for another 30 minutes. Strain the stock through a fine-mesh strainer.

In a large gumbo pot over medium-low heat, melt the butter and sauté the green onions for about 2 minutes. Add the flour, thyme, and garlic and sauté, stirring, until the flour turns light brown. Whisk in the crab stock, and simmer over medium heat for 10 minutes. Add the corn and continue to simmer for another 10 minutes. Add the cream while stirring, and then add the crabmeat. Stir to mix well and remove from the heat. Allow to rest and cool for 20 minutes, stirring periodically. Add the remaining ingredients, stir, and slowly reheat. Serve immediately.

Davis Bayou Shrimp and Okra Gumbo

Recipe courtesy of Ariel Taylor
Yield: 10 to 12 servings

This is a nicely thickened gumbo. However, more chicken stock may be added as needed to thin it. A large dollop of potato salad right in the center of each bowl of gumbo makes a delightful treat—with any gumbo, actually.

1½ cups all-purpose flour
1½ cups canola oil or butter
1½ cups chopped onions
1 cup chopped celery
½ cup chopped green bell peppers
4 cups chicken stock
5 cloves garlic, minced
¼ cup parsley, chopped
2 12-ounce cans diced tomatoes
3 cups sliced okra
3 bay leaves

2 tablespoons Worcestershire sauce
2 teaspoons basil
2 teaspoons oregano
Tabasco or Crystal hot sauce to
    taste
Salt and black pepper to taste
4 pounds fresh Mississippi claw blue
    crabmeat
4 pounds jumbo (U16/20) fresh
    Mississippi shrimp, peeled and
    deveined

In a large gumbo pot, combine the flour and oil or butter and cook over medium heat, stirring constantly to make a roux. When the roux turns a dark caramel color, add the onions, celery, and bell peppers and cook, stirring, for about 5 to 7 minutes. Add 2 cups chicken stock and reserve the rest. Bring to a strong simmer, cover, and cook for 15 minutes. Add the garlic and parsley and stir. Add the tomatoes, okra, bay leaves, Worcestershire, basil, and oregano and stir. Add the hot sauce and salt and pepper to taste. Add the crabmeat and stir. Cover, return to a simmer, and cook for another 20 minutes. More chicken stock may be added to replace any that evaporates. Thirty minutes prior to serving, add the shrimp and bring up to a low simmer. Stir periodically to keep any ingredients from sticking to the bottom. Serve over white rice.

Turnip Green Soup

Recipe courtesy of Dr. Bo Mayfield
Yield: 10 to 12 servings

A legend at many a Mississippi State tailgating party, this recipe has been perfected over two decades.

1 pound dry navy beans
1 large ham, bone in with scraps
8 smoked pork chops
2 tablespoons minced garlic
2 large onions, chopped
1 tablespoon Chef Paul
   Prudhomme's Vegetable Magic
   Seasoning Blend
3 to 4 bunches fresh turnip

greens (4 frozen boxes may be
  substituted)
2 10-ounce cans beef broth
2 10-ounce cans chicken broth
2 beef bouillon cubes
Salt and black pepper to taste
Tabasco or Crystal hot sauce to taste
4 large new potatoes, coarsely
  chopped

Turnip Green Soup and Jalapeno Cornbread fresh out of the oven, waiting on a bit of butter.

Rinse the navy beans, cover with water in a large bowl, and soak overnight. Or rinse the beans, cover with water in a pot, bring to a boil, remove from heat, and let sit for 1 hour.

In a second large pot, cover the bone-in ham and scraps with water. Add the pork chops and garlic. Bring to a boil. Reduce heat to medium low, cover, and simmer for 1 hour. Remove from heat and, when somewhat cool, skim off the fat with a ladle. Carefully remove the ham and pork chops and place on a cutting board. Remove the meat from the bone, coarsely chop, and set aside both the meat and the bones.

Bring the ham and garlic broth back up to a boil. Return the ham, pork, and bones to the pot liquor. Add the beans and remaining ingredients, except for the potatoes, and season to taste. Simmer over medium-low heat for 2 hours. Stir periodically. Add the potatoes and simmer for another 45 minutes. Serve in bowls over white or dirty rice, being careful not to serve the bones.

Bo's Posole

Recipe courtesy of Dr. Bo Mayfield
Yield: 10 to 12 servings

This posole can and should be served with as many of the following garnishes as desired—chopped onion, chopped avocado, lime wedges, chopped radish, chopped tomato, shredded lettuce, sour cream, salsa, and shredded cheese.

1 5-pound Boston butt
Salt and black pepper to taste
3 tablespoons peanut oil
2 medium onions, coarsely chopped
2 4-ounce cans green chilies,
   chopped
2 to 3 chipotle peppers in adobo
   sauce, chopped

1 tablespoon cumin
1 teaspoon ground coriander
1 teaspoon dried oregano
8 cups chicken broth
1 lime, quartered
4 15-ounce cans white hominy

Cut the Boston butt into 1- to 2-inch cubes and season with salt and pepper. In a large pot or Dutch oven over medium heat, heat the oil and brown the meat on all sides, about 5 to 7 minutes. Transfer the meat to a platter and set aside. Reduce the heat to medium low and add the onions. Cook until translucent, adding a bit more oil if necessary to keep the onions from burning. Return the pork to the pot and add the chilies, chipotle peppers, cumin, coriander, oregano, chicken broth, and lime quarters.

Rinse and drain the hominy in a colander, and then add to the pot. Mix thoroughly and bring to a low simmer. Cover and cook for 1½ to 2 hours until the meat is tender. Serve in bowls with garnishes.

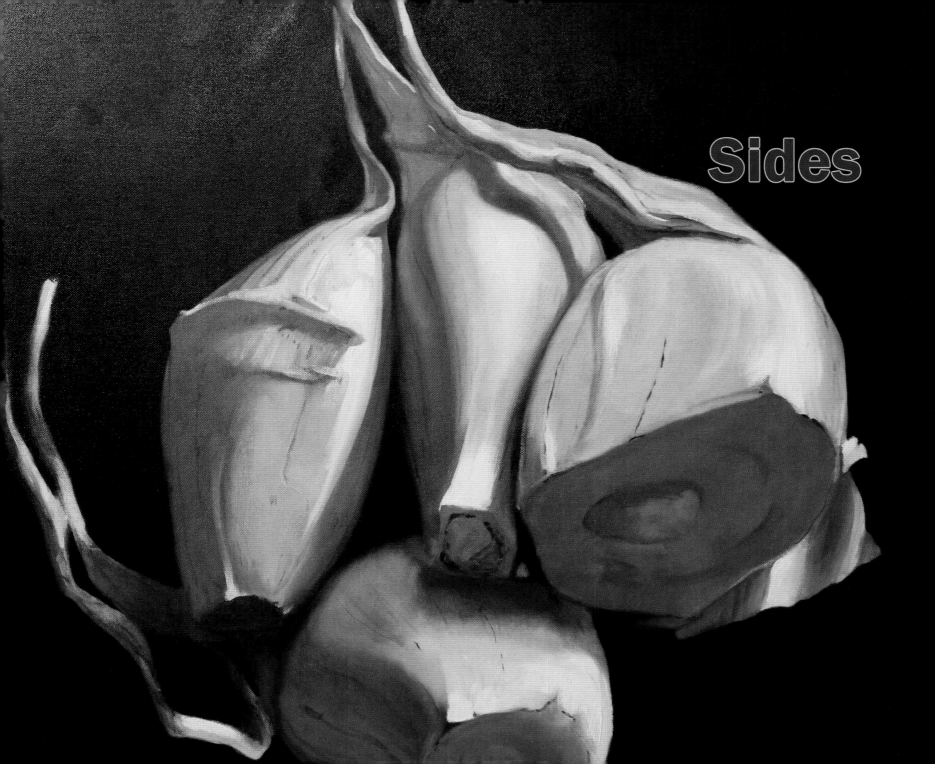

Sides

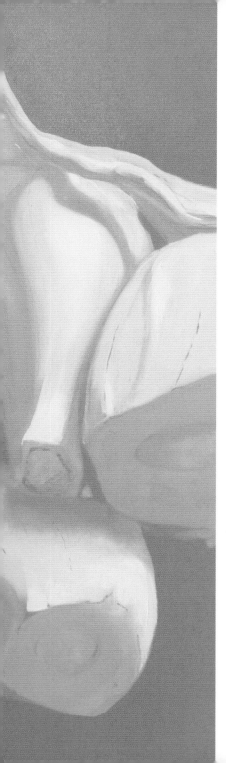

Minced Oyster Hushpuppies

Yield: 8 to 10 servings

Oil for frying
2 cups white cornmeal
1 cup all-purpose flour
1 tablespoon baking powder
2 teaspoons kosher salt
1 tablespoon black pepper
1 teaspoon cayenne pepper
1 cup buttermilk

1 egg
1 tablespoon prepared horseradish
1 quart Mississippi oysters, minced
½ bunch green onions, thinly sliced
½ cup minced yellow onion
4 cloves garlic, minced
1 tablespoon seeded and diced
   jalapeno

Preheat oil in the deep fryer to 350 degrees.

In a medium bowl, combine the dry ingredients and mix well. Add the buttermilk, egg, and horseradish and whisk well. Add the remaining ingredients and mix well.

Using 2 spoons, form the batter into a ball and lower the batter into the hot oil. Working in batches, repeat with more batter. Fry until golden brown, about 3 to 4 minutes. Be careful to not overcrowd the hushpuppies in the fryer.

Using tongs or a slotted spoon, remove them from the fryer and drain on a paper-towel-lined plate. Serve hot with Comeback Sauce (see index) or tartar sauce.

Pecan-Crusted Sweet Potato Pone

Yield: 8 to 10 servings

"Pone" is an old-school and very Southern term for bread or cake that originated from a Native American word. This particular dish is widely known today as "sweet potato crunch."

4 large sweet potatoes, peeled and
   sliced
4½ ounces unsalted butter
1¾ cups sugar
⅓ cup whole milk
2½ tablespoons cornstarch
1 tablespoon cinnamon

1 tablespoon pure vanilla extract
2 teaspoons lemon juice
¼ teaspoon nutmeg
2 large eggs
2 cups pecans
½ cup confectioners' sugar

Preheat the oven to 350 degrees.

Bring the sweet potatoes to a boil in a large pot of salted water and cook until soft. Drain well and mash with 4 ounces butter, 1½ cups sugar, milk, cornstarch, cinnamon, vanilla extract, lemon juice, and nutmeg. Allow to cool. Slightly beat in the eggs and set aside.

Toss the pecans in ½ ounce melted butter and ¼ cup sugar. Transfer the sweet potato mixture to an 8x8 casserole dish and sprinkle the pecans on top. Bake for 1 hour. Begin checking periodically after 45 minutes with a toothpick. If the dish is firm and the toothpick comes out clean, remove from the oven. Dust with the confectioners' sugar.

This dish can be served warm from the oven, sliced into squares at room temperature, or even cold.

"Pralined" Sweet Potatoes

Yield: 8 to 10 servings

¾ cup dark brown sugar
¼ cup sugar
12 tablespoons butter
Juice of 1 lemon
1 tablespoon salt

1 teaspoon vanilla extract
¼ teaspoon allspice
½ teaspoon cinnamon
6 large sweet potatoes, peeled and
   sliced

In a large saucepan over medium heat, combine all of the ingredients except for the sweet potatoes. Stir until the sugar has dissolved and is no longer grainy. If the mixture becomes too thick, add a little water to thin it out.

Add the potatoes and cook, stirring, for 10 minutes, until they begin to soften. Once soft, stir and mash the potatoes, but leave some of them intact. When the potatoes begin to stick to the pan and become a light caramel color, remove from the heat and transfer to a serving platter. Serve alongside turkey or pork.

Caramelized "Sweet Pads"

Yield: 6 to 8 servings

While attending culinary school in New York, Chef Matthew rapidly discovered that not only had no one in Poughkeepsie ever heard of a sweet potato called a "sweet pad" but neither had any of his fellow Southerners. The chef's mother quickly clarified for him that he had been unable to say "sweet potato" as a child and the family had adopted his pronunciation of "sweet pads." Needless to say, Chef had to go hat in hand to apologize to several of his classmates and instructors for "explaining" to them that they knew nothing about the South. This is a tried-and-true recipe for simple caramelized "sweet pads" and works well with most any protein.

¼ cup bacon fat or butter
2 large sweet potatoes, peeled and
    sliced into ⅓-inch-thick rounds
Kosher salt to taste

In a cast-iron skillet over medium heat, melt the bacon fat or butter. Add the thick sweet potato slices. Lightly add 1 or 2 scant teaspoons salt. Cook the potatoes until they are well caramelized, about 7 to 9 minutes per side. Remove from the heat and serve.

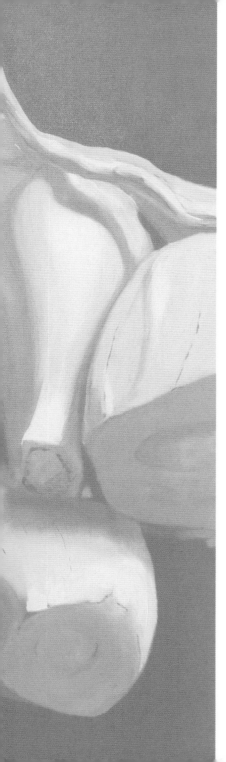

The Perfect Grit Girl Grits

Recipe courtesy of Georgeanne Ross
Yield: 4 servings

Georgeanne Maupin Ross, better known as the Grit Girl, started grinding grits outside of Oxford in 2001 after her husband restored a 1912 Fairbanks Morse flywheel engine. Ms. Georgeanne explains, "When it was completed, he brought it home to show me. It was neat, big and red, but what the heck was it for?" Her husband then restored a 1910 Meadows Stone Grist Mill, and the next thing they knew, they were producing stone-ground cornmeal, which leads to grits and masa. Since then, Ms. Georgeanne has been producing cornmeal, grits, masa, and polenta using corn from a local farmer every other Sunday to order. Her client list includes virtually every high-end restaurant in Mississippi and many in Memphis. Ms. Georgeanne will ship her pure corn products just about anywhere—and she is quite the hoot to talk to. Here's her recipe for simply the best grits you've ever eaten.

2 cups chicken broth
½ cup heavy cream
1 cup Original Grit Girl stone-ground
   yellow grits

In a large saucepan, combine the chicken broth and cream. Bring to a boil. Stir in the Original Grit Girl Grits. Cover, reduce the heat, and simmer for 20 minutes. Stir often. Remove from the heat and serve.

Chef's Note: For the perfect cheese grits, add 2 cups shredded yellow or white cheddar cheese. Be creative and try different types of cheese—how about Beemster cheese grits? When the grits are soft, after about 15 minutes, add the cheese. When it is melted, serve and enjoy!

Fried Grits with Crumbled Bacon and Jalapenos

Yield: 6 to 8 servings

2 cups chicken broth
½ cup heavy cream
½ teaspoon salt
½ teaspoon black pepper
1 cup Original Grit Girl stone-ground
   yellow grits
6 slices bacon, cooked
1 jalapeno, minced

2 eggs
Heavy splash of half-and-half
1 cup all-purpose flour
1 cup Original Grit Girl masa or corn
   flour
Peanut oil for frying
Confectioners' sugar for dusting

In a large saucepan, bring the chicken broth, cream, salt, and pepper to a boil. Add the grits. Reduce the heat to a simmer and stir periodically until it reaches a thick consistency. If it becomes too thick, add a splash of milk to thin it out.

Remove from the heat. Crumble the cooled bacon and jalapenos into the grits and mix well. Pour the grits into a baking dish, cover with aluminum foil, and let cool for a few minutes before transferring to the refrigerator. Refrigerate for at least 4 hours or until hardened.

Place the flour in a shallow bowl. In another shallow bowl, whisk together the eggs and half-and-half. Place the masa in a third shallow bowl. Remove the baking dish with the grits from the refrigerator and slice into rectangles or squares.

In a skillet over medium-high heat, add just enough peanut oil to cover the surface of the pan. Dredge the grit cakes in the flour and shake off the excess. Then dip into the egg wash and dredge in the masa.

Cook, in batches if necessary, until they turn golden brown on all sides. Transfer the grit cakes to a paper-towel-lined plate to drain and then repeat the process with the remaining cakes. To serve, place 1 or 2 of the grit cakes on each plate and dust lightly with confectioners' sugar.

Snap Beans with Apple-Smoked Bacon

Recipe courtesy of Elizabeth Charbonnet
Yield: 6 to 8 servings

This side dish pairs well with nearly anything, from chicken to pork to fish.

12 tablespoons butter
1 pound apple-smoked bacon,
   coarsely chopped
1½ to 2 pounds fresh snap beans
1 large onion, thinly sliced

6-8 small red potatoes, halved or
   quartered
1 teaspoon fresh tarragon leaves
½ teaspoon Pickapeppa sauce
1 teaspoon fresh thyme leaves

In a Dutch oven, melt the butter over low heat, then add the bacon, beans, and onions. Increase the heat to medium, cover, and cook for 30 minutes, stirring often. If the beans begin to stick to the bottom, add butter as needed.

Reduce the heat to low and add the potatoes and spices. Cook, covered, stirring often, for about 20 minutes or until the potatoes are soft enough to stick a fork into them. Remove from the heat and serve immediately.

(Photographs courtesy of Matthew Mayfield)

Turnip Greens with Pickled Pork and Lazy Magnolia Southern Pecan Beer

Yield: 6 to 8 servings

½ pound apple-smoked bacon
1 medium onion, chopped
1 large bunch turnip greens, washed, large stems removed, cut in a chiffonade
Salt and black pepper to taste
2 cups chicken stock
1 12-ounce bottle Lazy Magnolia Southern Pecan beer
½ tablespoon minced garlic
2 tablespoons Worcestershire sauce
2 tablespoons butter
1 tablespoon dark brown sugar
1½ pounds pickled pork, cubed
1 teaspoon Tabasco or Crystal hot sauce
½ cup shredded smoked Gouda cheese

In a large skillet over low heat, cook the bacon to render the fat. Transfer the bacon to a paper-towel-lined plate and set aside. In a large skillet, sauté the onions in the bacon fat until brown and caramelized.

Add the chiffonade of greens and cook for 3 to 4 minutes. Season with salt and pepper. Add the stock, beer, garlic, and Worcestershire and cook until the greens are tender, approximately 15 minutes.

In a separate heavy pan, combine the butter and brown sugar. As the mixture starts to bubble, add the pickled pork cubes and toss to coat. Chop the bacon and add. Cook, stirring, until the pork is brown on all sides.

Add the pork to the cooked greens and simmer for 1 to 2 minutes. Add the hot sauce and adjust the seasoning. Top each serving with Gouda. Serve immediately.

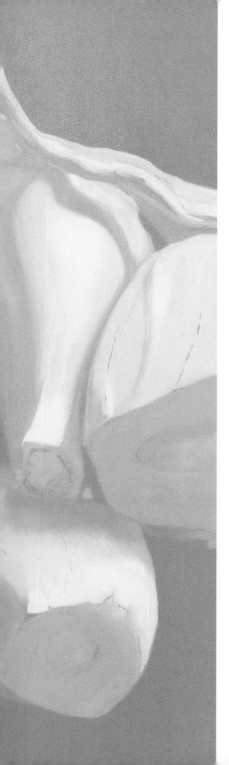

Channel Marker Brussels Sprouts with Apple-Smoked Bacon

Yield: 6 to 8 servings

3 tablespoons extra-virgin olive oil
1 heaping tablespoon honey
1 tablespoon sugarcane vinegar
2 teaspoons Bonney's hot sauce or
   Tabasco
6 cloves garlic, coarsely chopped
1 pound fresh Brussels sprouts,
   stemmed and halved

1 small red onion, diced
1 small turnip, peeled and chopped
4 tablespoons butter
Salt and black pepper to taste
1 pound apple-smoked bacon,
   chopped
¼ cup grated parmesan cheese

Preheat the oven to 350 degrees.

Place the olive oil, honey, vinegar, hot sauce, and garlic in a bowl and mix well. Add the Brussels sprouts, onion, and turnip. Melt the butter in a cast-iron skillet over medium heat. When the butter starts to bubble, add the Brussels sprouts mixture, salt, pepper, and bacon and stir to coat the sprouts with the butter. Place the skillet into the oven and cook for 40 to 45 minutes, stirring once halfway through the cooking time. Remove from the oven, sprinkle with the grated parmesan, and serve.

Vidalia Onion Pie

Recipe courtesy of Ruth Hanna Victoria Streed Ramsay
Yield: 10 servings

This old-school dish can totally be riffed on. Think of adding spicy Italian sausage or even crabmeat as a protein—just don't call it a pot pie. Consider it an open culinary canvas.

8 tablespoons butter
2 pounds Vidalia onions, coarsely
  chopped
1 cup sour cream
3 eggs, beaten
½ teaspoon black pepper

½ teaspoon thyme
¼ teaspoon salt
Dash or 2 or 3 of Tabasco, Crystal,
  or your favorite hot sauce
2 9-inch unbaked pie shells
¼ cup shaved parmesan cheese

Preheat oven to 450 degrees.

In a cast-iron skillet over medium heat, melt the butter. Add the onions and cook until nearly translucent, about 20 minutes. Once the onions are tender, lower the heat, add the sour cream and eggs, and stir. Add the spices and continue stirring. Remove from heat and pour the mixture into the pie shells. Generously sprinkle the pies with the shaved parmesan cheese and place into the oven.

Bake for 20 minutes. Reduce the heat to 325 degrees and cook for another 20 minutes. Remove from oven and serve.

Summer Squash and Cornbread Jalapeno Dressing

Yield: 8 to 10 servings

8 to 10 yellow squash, chopped
4 medium yellow onions, chopped
1 medium Vidalia onion, chopped
1 box Jiffy cornbread, baked and
  crumbled
6 slices apple-smoked bacon,
  cooked and crumbled

2 10-ounce cans cream of chicken
  soup
2 jalapenos, seeded and minced
4 tablespoons butter, melted
1 teaspoon ground thyme
Salt and black pepper to taste

Preheat the oven to 350 degrees.

Bring a medium pot of water to a boil. Add the squash and onions, and cook for 5 minutes. Remove from the heat, drain the squash and onions, and set aside to briefly cool. Using a fork or potato masher, coarsely mash the squash and onions. They should still be fairly recognizable.

In the same pot, add the remaining ingredients and mix together. Add the squash. Grease a 9x13 casserole dish and bake the mixture for 25 minutes. Serve alongside pork, turkey, duck, or your favorite roast.

Peas in a Roux

Recipe courtesy of Winifred Berthelot
Yield: 4 servings

This is an old-school side dish served by many home chefs in South Louisiana that quickly made the jump over to the coast. While this dish may have faded from popularity, for some households it remains a weekly and holiday staple—and for delicious reasons.

4 tablespoons butter
½ cup all-purpose flour
1 12-ounce can sweet peas
1 cup cooked white or dirty rice

In a medium pot over medium-low heat, melt the butter. Add the flour. Using a flat-bottomed roux paddle or whisk, stir the roux until it is a dark chocolate color. Immediately pour in the can of peas, including the water in the can, taking care to avoid scalding, and stir well to combine. Once the peas are hot, serve ladled over the rice and next to any protein.

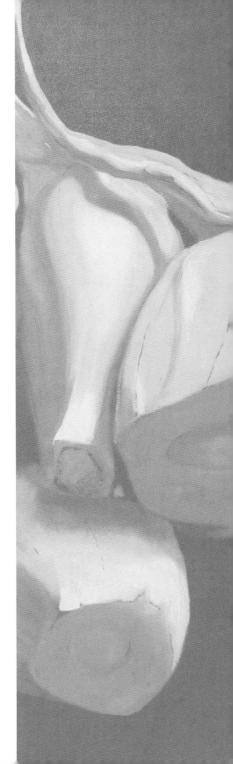

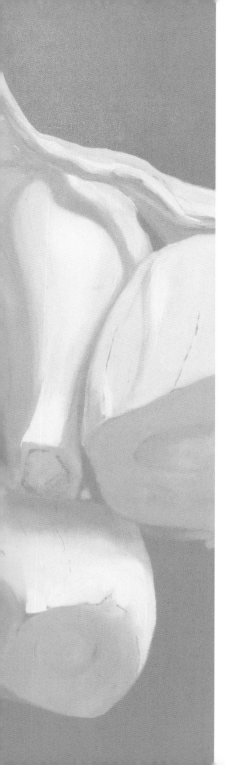

Fried Okra

Yield: 6 to 8 servings

Bacon fat can be substituted for the oil in order to bring the okra to a whole other level of deliciousness.

2 pounds fresh okra, washed, stemmed, and cut into ½-inch pieces
1½ cups Original Grit Girl cornmeal
Oil for frying

1 teaspoon salt
1 teaspoon freshly ground black pepper
¼ teaspoon cayenne pepper

Combine the okra and cornmeal in a large resealable bag. Shake to thoroughly coat the okra. Heat the oil in a large cast-iron skillet. Test the heat by dropping a bit of cornmeal into the oil. When hot, add the okra in batches. Fry until the okra is crispy looking, about 5 minutes.

Transfer the okra to a paper-towel-lined plate to drain. Season with salt, pepper, and cayenne. Serve hot.

Fresh okra at a farmers' market, which have become common throughout Mississippi. The state is not only blessed with incredible seafood, but the interior is ideal for farming, with a long growing season and many farms still family owned and operated.

Green Rice with Okra, Pimento, and Parmesan Cheese

Yield: 10 to 12 servings

2 cups uncooked Delta Blues white
   rice
8 tablespoons butter
½ pound fresh okra, washed,
   stemmed, and cut into ¼-inch
   pieces
1 green pepper, diced
2 4-ounce bottles chopped

   pimentos, undrained
2 medium onions, chopped
1 cup fresh parsley, chopped
1 cup chopped celery
4 cups chicken broth
½ cup freshly grated parmesan
   cheese

Preheat the oven to 350 degrees.

Cook the rice and set aside.

In a cast-iron skillet over medium-low heat, melt 1 tablespoon butter. Add the okra and cook for 6 minutes. Remove from heat and pour into a large mixing bowl.

Melt the remaining butter. Add the rice, remaining vegetables, melted butter, and chicken broth to the okra. Mix well. Pour the mixture into a greased casserole dish and loosely cover with aluminum foil.

Bake for 45 minutes or until the liquid is absorbed and rice is tender. Remove and immediately generously dust the green rice with the parmesan cheese. Serve immediately as a side dish.

Rice may not sound as though it can be artisanal, but look out onto the Delta Blues Rice fields . . . it's hard to imagine how you couldn't put any rice from these fields onto your table. (Photograph by Rory Doyle)

The Junction Mac and Cheese

Yield: 10 to 12 servings

Many variations of cheese could work in this simple dish. Try cheddar, goat, Roquefort, parmesan, or even a combination—but we prefer the color combination of maroon paprika and white cheeses, for obvious reasons. This is delicious hot or cold.

1 pound macaroni	University Vallagret cheese,
1 quart heavy cream	shredded
½ teaspoon minced garlic	Salt and black pepper to taste
2 pounds Mississippi State	2 tablespoons paprika

Cook the macaroni in boiling salted water until half-cooked. Drain and keep warm.

In a heavy-bottomed pot, combine the cream and garlic. Bring to a simmer over low heat, cooking until it reduces by ⅓. Add the half-cooked pasta, mix well, and let the cream reduce by another ⅓.

Stir in ½ of the cheese. Season to taste with salt and pepper. Serve with the remaining cheese sprinkled on top and then generously dust with the paprika. Store in a resealable container.

Blue Crab and Cognac Casserole

Yield: 10 servings

12 tablespoons butter
1¼ cups coarsely chopped green
   onions
1½ cups heavy cream
½ cup whole milk
1 tablespoon dried parsley
½ cup all-purpose flour

1¼ teaspoons salt
1 teaspoon white pepper
1 tablespoon cognac
3 pounds fresh Mississippi lump
   blue crabmeat, twice picked
5 cups grated Mississippi State
   University sharp cheddar cheese

Preheat oven to 325 degrees.

In a cast-iron skillet over medium heat, melt the butter. Add the green onions, cream, milk, parsley, flour, salt, and pepper, and bring to a simmer. Remove from heat. Add the cognac, crabmeat, and 2½ cups cheese and mix well. Pour into a greased shallow baking dish.

Transfer to the oven and bake until bubbly, about 20 minutes. Remove from the oven and sprinkle the remaining cheese on top. Serve when the cheese has melted.

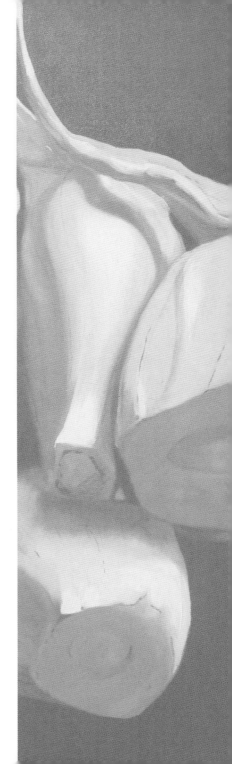

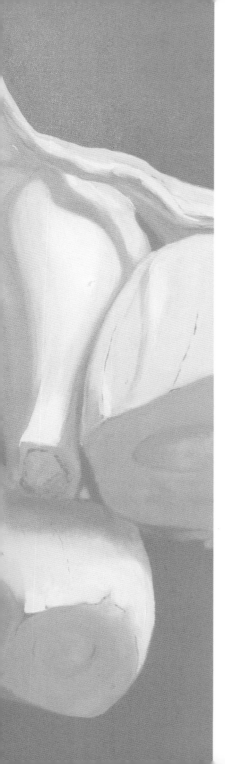

Summer Squash, Shrimp, and Blue Crab Casserole

Recipe courtesy of Jocelyn Mayfield, Jocelyn's Restaurant, Ocean Springs
Yield: 8 to 10 servings

8 tablespoons butter
8 to 10 yellow squash, sliced into half-moons
2 large yellow onions, chopped
1 pound medium (U41/50) fresh Mississippi brown shrimp, peeled and deveined
½ pound fresh Mississippi lump blue crabmeat, twice picked

1 cup grated Mississippi State University sharp cheddar cheese
1 cup Ritz crackers, coarsely crushed
1 egg, beaten
Salt and black pepper to taste

Preheat the oven to 425 degrees.

In a cast-iron skillet over medium heat, melt the butter. Add the squash and onions, and sauté until the onions become translucent, about 8 minutes. Reduce the heat to medium low and add the shrimp.

When the shrimp become pink, about 2 minutes, remove from the heat. Add the crabmeat and cheese and mix thoroughly. Blend in the crushed crackers and the egg, and season.

Place the cast-iron skillet into the oven, or grease a 9x13 casserole dish and add the squash and seafood mixture. Cook for 15 minutes or until the top begins to brown. Serve alongside pork, turkey, or duck.

Beulah's Drop Biscuits

Recipe courtesy of Beulah Lee Martin Smith
Yield: 10 biscuits

2 cups all-purpose flour
2 teaspoons baking powder
½ teaspoon baking soda
1 teaspoon sugar

¾ teaspoon salt
8 tablespoons butter, melted
1 cup buttermilk

Preheat the oven to 475 degrees.

In a mixing bowl, combine all of the dry ingredients. Add the butter and buttermilk and mix thoroughly, until the dough becomes lumpy and pulls away from the sides of the bowl. Scoop out about ¼ cup for each biscuit and drop onto a wax-paper-lined baking sheet.

Transfer to the oven and bake for 12 to 14 minutes or until golden brown.

Enjoy with butter or jam.

Momma's Yeast Rolls

Yield: 10 servings

2 cups whole milk, "warm like a baby"
2¼ teaspoons active dry yeast
½ cup sugar
1 teaspoon salt
¼ cup shortening

1 hen egg, also known as a "yard egg"
5 cups all-purpose flour
Oil
Melted butter

Preheat the oven to 350 degrees.

In a mixing bowl, combine the warm milk and the yeast. Stir in the sugar and allow it to rest until it begins to bubble, about 15 minutes. Add the salt, shortening, and egg and mix well. Add 2 or 3 cups flour and mix well, using your hands or a wooden spoon. Slowly add the remaining flour and mix.

Cover the dough with a kitchen towel. Set aside in a warm spot in the kitchen and allow the dough to double in size. Punch the dough down and then knead it well. Brush it with oil so it will not dry out. Set it aside, covered, and allow it to rise again.

Bounce the dough on a cutting board in order to get all the air out. Using a rolling pin, roll out the dough until the length and width of the rolling pin, about ¼ inch thick. Pinch off a 2-inch square of the dough for each roll and place on a lined baking sheet. Brush each roll with melted butter and transfer to the oven.

Bake for 12 to 15 minutes or until golden brown.

Enjoy.

Biloxi's Hurricane Hunters

Maj. Brad Boudreaux banked his Air Force C-130 and immediately headed south after takeoff. Below him, in the Intracoastal Waterway, were legions of boats ranging from 60-foot sportfishing charters to 20-foot sailboats fleeing what he was about to fly into—the eye of a hurricane in the Gulf of Mexico.

As a pilot for the legendary Hurricane Hunters out of Keesler Air Force Base in Biloxi, Mississippi and a native of Covington, Louisiana, Major Boudreaux knows all too well the periodic hazards of the Gulf Coast boating life. He also understands that he couldn't live anywhere else. Boudreaux transferred from flying B-52 bombers to the Hurricane Hunters in 2007 specifically to get access to the water and return to the Gulf Coast lifestyle.

"Since I can remember, I have always been on a boat. I was driving boats before I could legally drive a car." Boudreaux leans against his trailered 24-foot Glacier Bay. He is one of those guys who is either "boat rich" or "boat poor" depending on

Hurricane Hunter Maj. Brad Boudreaux's son wakeboards on the Tchoutacabouffa River in Biloxi.

how you look at it— he has 5. He could tell boating stories all weekend. "I started waterskiing when I was 6 years old on the Tchefuncte River in Louisiana and I was slaloming by the time I was 9. Now I have my kids out here wakeboarding 3 to 4 times a week on the Tchoutacabouffa River behind our house in Biloxi."

The Hurricane Hunters formed in 1943 following a barroom dare between 2 Air Force pilots. Their mission is to fly directly into the deadliest winds and weather of Atlantic-season hurricanes and take a multitude of readings. The Hurricane Hunters' modified C-130s are filled with specialized equipment that helps to gauge storm speed, direction, intensity, potential landfalls, and, if necessary, evacuations throughout the Southeastern and Gulf coasts of the United States. All of the pilots, crews, and ground-support personnel live in hurricane country—their mission is personal.

Boudreaux adds, "When storms build in the Gulf, that means I'm working, and so for my family, we have a plan that we have to set in motion out of necessity way before anyone else and that, of course, includes a plan for securing and trailering the boats."

On one flight into a tropical storm that was rapidly intensifying into a Category 1 hurricane, Boudreaux had one of his most dangerous experiences on a mission. "This storm was rapidly building with heavy rains, hail, turbulence, and lightning. We started experiencing heavy downdrafts from a severe thunderstorm, and a mesocyclone—basically an airborne tornado—suddenly developed in front of us and we couldn't evade. It first tried to turn the airplane upside down, and when we wouldn't let it do that, it threw us into a nosedive."

Maj. Sean Cross knows these experiences all too well, both in the air and on the ground. He and his family went through Hurricane Katrina in Biloxi and were transferred to Atlanta along with the entire Hurricane Hunter squadron, who continued to operate without missing a beat even as their homes and property and the base were laid to waste. "Our home was damaged. I mean, basically, if you don't live on the water down here, you can see it. Everyone was affected."

Major Cross grew up in New Orleans trawling and shrimping with his Paw Paw on a Lafitte skiff, eventually inheriting the boat. As he got older, he moved on to Chaparrals and WaveRunners and today runs a Sea Ray 260 Sundancer that he and his wife pleasure boat on throughout the Gulf's barrier islands. "We keep the boat in Destin, Florida during the summer months and my wife and I spend a lot of time out at Crab Island in the Destin Pass. We live for those long weekends."

As with any military organization, there is a lot of camaraderie. Unit cohesion exists whether on duty or not, and that includes on the water for these Air Force pilots. Major Boudreaux and Major Cross both live on the same river in Biloxi. Cross explains, "Most people walk their neighborhoods and see their neighbors, but here on the Gulf Coast we take the WaveRunners out with the kids and meet up with the other water bugs. The kids enjoy themselves and the adults stop in for some type of refreshment."

Hurricane Hunter Lt. Col. Jeff Ragusa was born in Baton Rouge, Louisiana, grew up waterskiing on the False and Tickfaw rivers, and today lives in Biloxi.

Hurricane Hunters. (Photograph courtesy of the United States Air Force)

"You will feel out of place here if you don't fish and certainly if you don't boat."

Lieutenant Colonel Ragusa keeps his Bayliner in dry storage at the Keesler Air Force Base marina and is able to leave his "office" and be on the water in 30 minutes. He and his wife waterski but primarily take their high-school-aged son and his friends out kneeboarding. Their real passion is waterfront dining. "We love finding restaurants along the coast where we can take a sunset cruise, dock up, and have dinner. We go as far as Gulfport and Ocean Springs along the ICW, but the Biloxi back bay has so many restaurants with docks and it is so convenient that we are out there at least once a week."

Like any division of the U.S. military, all of the men and women who constitute the Hurricane Hunters execute and understand their mission, but there is an especially personal aspect to what these crews do. Ragusa explains, "Our unit has a certain advantage that most units do not have and that I wish they did. We live in this community here in Mississippi and on the Gulf Coast and our mission directly affects our neighbors. Everyone in the military has people and individuals that come up and thank them for their service, but here we have people that come up to us in the grocery store or at our son's school and thank us for what we do not only for this country but for our local community."

Sauces

Solitario

Jezebel Sauce

Yield: About 7 cups

1 18-ounce jar pineapple preserves
1 18-ounce jar apple jelly
2 5-ounce jars prepared horseradish

½ cup Coleman's dry mustard
1 tablespoon fresh-ground black
  pepper

In a mixing bowl, combine all of the ingredients and whisk thoroughly. Store in Mason jars or cleaned condiment jars. Using an indelible marker, write the date on the lids or outsides of the containers, and refrigerate for up to 1 month. Serve on ham, pork, or roast beef sandwiches or as a glaze or dipping sauce for the same.

Bush's Garlic Aioli

Recipe courtesy of Bush LeBourgeois
Yield: ½ cup

1 large egg
1 tablespoon water
2 teaspoons kosher salt

6 cloves garlic
¼ cup canola oil

In a blender, add the egg, water, salt, and garlic. Pulse the blender, and slowly drizzle in the oil until the mixture becomes thick and forms an emulsion. If necessary, add more oil until you have reached the desired consistency.

Desporte's Cocktail Sauce

Recipe courtesy of Sean Desporte, Desporte & Sons Seafood Market & Deli, Biloxi
Yield: 2 cups

1 cup homemade or store-bought
   mayonnaise
½ cup ketchup
1 tablespoon Creole mustard
1 hard-boiled egg, minced
1 tablespoon minced yellow onion

1 tablespoon prepared horseradish
4 cloves garlic, minced
1 teaspoon Tony Chachere's Creole
   Seasoning
1 teaspoon black pepper
1 teaspoon lemon pepper

In a mixing bowl, combine all of the ingredients and whisk thoroughly. Store in Mason jars or cleaned condiment jars. Using an indelible marker, write the date on the lids or outsides of the containers, and refrigerate for up to 2 weeks. Serve as a dipping sauce for fried seafood or raw oysters.

Comeback Sauce

Yield: 1 cup

This is a very versatile sauce that can be enjoyed even as a salad dressing. Hot sauce may be added to give it an extra kick.

½ cup chili sauce
½ cup Duke's mayonnaise
¼ cup canola oil
1 teaspoon black pepper

1 teaspoon garlic powder
1 teaspoon prepared horseradish
2 teaspoons lemon juice

In a mixing bowl, combine all of the ingredients and whisk thoroughly. Store in Mason jars or cleaned condiment jars. Using an indelible marker, write the date on the lids or outsides of the containers, and refrigerate for up to 6 months and at least 24 hours before using. Serve as a dipping sauce for fried or boiled seafood or even saltines.

Rotisserie Dressing

Yield: 2 cups

This is a very versatile sauce that can be enjoyed even as a salad dressing. You may substitute your favorite mayonnaise for the sour cream, but then omit the sugar.

1 cup sour cream
2 tablespoons sugar
½ cup extra-virgin olive oil
1 cup chili sauce or ketchup
1 heaping tablespoon minced yellow
  onion
1 teaspoon kosher salt
½ teaspoon fresh-ground black
  pepper

2 tablespoons cold water
1 tablespoon Worcestershire sauce
4 or 5 dashes Bonney's hot sauce or
  Tabasco
2 cloves garlic, minced
1 tablespoon dry mustard
1 teaspoon prepared horseradish

In a mixing bowl, combine all of the ingredients and whisk thoroughly. Store in Mason jars or cleaned condiment jars. Using an indelible marker, write the date on the lids or outsides of the containers, and refrigerate for up to 6 months and at least 24 hours before using. Serve as a dipping sauce for fried or boiled seafood.

Tartar Sauce

Yield: 2½ cups

2 cups homemade or store-bought
　mayonnaise
4 tablespoons minced dill pickles
1 teaspoon fresh tarragon
½ teaspoon Coleman's dry mustard

2 teaspoons pureed onion
½ teaspoon cayenne pepper
1 teaspoon lemon juice
Salt and black pepper to taste

In a mixing bowl, combine all of the ingredients and whisk thoroughly. Store in
Mason jars or cleaned condiment jars. Using an indelible marker, write the date
on the lids or outsides of the containers, and refrigerate for up to 6 months.

The Chandeleur Boats

Dean Gladney has been running his 65-foot custom charter boat, the *Beachwater II*, south and west into the Mississippi Sound from Biloxi since the 1980s. Eight other large vessels similar to Gladney's are known as "Chandeleur boats," and they make the unique run to Louisiana's Chandeleur Islands and the Breton National Wildlife Refuge for what Gladney calls a "paradise of fishing."

Also known as "motherships," what's distinctive about the Biloxi Chandeleur boats is that they act as a mobile headquarters, with 6 or more 14-foot skiffs loaded onboard as well as the ability to tow their charter's personal boats for long, 3-day tours of nonstop fishing and camaraderie for up to 12 people. Onboard each spacious boat, with the feel of a rustic fishing camp, Gladney's three-man crew cleans the day's hauls of redfish, speckled trout, and flounder and cooks some of the finest Gulf Coast suppers imaginable. Everything is taken care of—all you have to do is catch the fish.

"The Chandeleurs really are a paradise even though they have been ravaged by hurricanes over the last 30 years and are a quarter of their size now." At 22 years old, Gladney started working as a deckhand for his father in 1979, and his institutional knowledge of fishing in the area is unrivaled. "There are so many coves, little bayous, points, and grassy habitats out there that are magnets for these fish, and when they turn on, boy, do they turn on. In the late summer, we get my charters out on the Gulf-side beaches for surf fishing."

Chip Chandler stands ready to defend his redfish recipe against anyone's.

Ideal for large groups of old friends or families, the motherships offer a spectacular way to spend a long weekend. These rarely visited areas are out of cell-phone range, and the large stern deck or bow are perfect for sunsets or stargazing as well as socializing. Down below, poker games run late into the night. In the spring, thousands of pelicans and other seabirds come to the island chain for nesting, and the shoreline is ideal for beachcombing. The real goal, however, is the fishing.

Running a little skiff out from the mothership into the marsh shallows with an ice chest and then drifting along the shore until you find that one perfect spot where the fish start biting is a unique experience. Never far from the floating base, it's truly

a relaxed fishing expedition, without the worries of returning to the boat launch and getting home in time for supper.

The season lasts from April until November, and it's best to book early. The *Beachwater II* and the other Chandeleur boats fill up quickly, with many repeat customers extending their trips by staying at the casinos adjacent to the marinas. Reflecting on his years onboard the *Beachwater II*, Gladney adds, "It's really just been a good life out here on the water and helping so many people see and explore these islands with me."

It was a slow fishing day, so behind the scenes, most of the other guys took a photo with this fellow's fish.

Chip's *Beachwater II* Fried Redfish

Recipe courtesy of Chip Chandler, Beachwater II
Yield: 8 servings

3 eggs
1 tablespoon Sriracha
2 teaspoons Old Bay seasoning
2 teaspoons Louisiana or Crystal hot
   sauce
2 cups whole milk
2 tablespoons black pepper
2 tablespoons Creole mustard
2 tablespoons yellow mustard
2 tablespoons prepared horseradish

6 pounds fresh Mississippi or
   Louisiana redfish filets, skinned
   and cut into large chunks
4 cups all-purpose flour
Salt and black pepper to taste
4 cups seasoned fish fry
Oil for frying
Comeback or Tartar Sauce (see
   index)

In a large bowl, prepare the egg wash by mixing together the eggs, Sriracha, Old Bay, hot sauce, milk, 2 tablespoons pepper, mustards, and horseradish. Soak the redfish in the egg wash for 10 minutes. Transfer to a paper-towel-lined plate.

Place the flour, salt, and pepper in a shallow bowl. Pour the egg mixture into another shallow bowl. Place the fish fry in a third shallow bowl.

Preheat oil in a deep fryer to 375 degrees.

Dredge the redfish in the flour and shake off the excess. Then dip into the egg wash and dredge in the fish fry. Carefully place into the hot oil. If using a smaller pot for frying, do this in batches. Remove when the redfish is golden brown and floating in the oil, about 5 minutes or less, depending on the size of the redfish chunks. Serve immediately with Comeback or Tartar Sauce for dipping.

At rest.

The Royal Reds

Shrimp has always been considered the "cheap" meat on the Gulf Coast. Thumb through decades-old coast cookbooks and you're more likely to find recipes for shrimp than any other sort of protein—and not much has changed today. Generations of families have plied the nutrient-rich bays and estuaries of Louisiana, Mississippi, Alabama, and Florida where they meet the Gulf of Mexico, for the natural abundance of brown and white shrimp. However, there is a shrimp species on the Gulf Coast that is incredibly difficult to come by but highly desired by locals and the few tourists in on the secret—the Royal Reds.

Found along the continental shelf in deep water, these prized and naturally ruby red shrimp rarely make it to the finer dining establishments in New Orleans. Most are sold directly off the trawlers the minute they come into dock. Chefs and home cooks have to be vigilant in order to find a source, let alone a consistent supply when the Royal Reds are in season.

The Gulf Coast's brown and white shrimp are well known throughout the country, with the Northern Gulf Coast supplying 70 percent of the shrimp catch. Discovered in the 1950s by government scientists trawling the deep depths of the Gulf, the Royal Reds are entirely different from their common cousins, who prefer the shallower coastal waters. The Royals enjoy the cooler water temperatures found at least a half-mile down, and their entire life cycle happens at these great depths.

While of similar size to the standard Gulf Coast shrimp, this deepwater species has a sweeter flavor and a texture that has been compared to lobster. Their relatively unknown status and scarcity in the market and on restaurant menus are directly attributed to the distance shrimpers must travel to find them. The first shrimp catches on the Gulf Coast were harvested using horses pulling nets through the estuaries, and this was eventually followed by shallow-draft luggers under sail. Today, though, the added fuel costs for trawlers to head sometimes as far as 60 miles offshore, and the extreme *Beautiful Royal Reds boiled to perfection.*

123

depths needed for their nets, make most shrimpers stay close to the coast for the lucrative brown and white shrimp.

There are exceptions. Most of the Royal Reds are pulled in off the coast of Alabama and, to some degree, the lower Gulf Coast of Florida and the Keys. During their fall season, the Royal Reds appear in many beachside restaurants in Orange Beach and Gulf Shores, Alabama, and select waterfront dining establishments in South Florida. Be careful, though. No shrimp should be poached or boiled for longer than a few minutes, but the Royals can take even less time, otherwise they become gummy.

Inevitably, as fuel costs decrease and word spreads about this Gulf Coast delicacy, shrimpers will react to market demand and the Royal Reds will become more common. Today, though, enjoying the saltier and more lobster-like texture of the Royal Reds should be considered a culinary badge of honor.

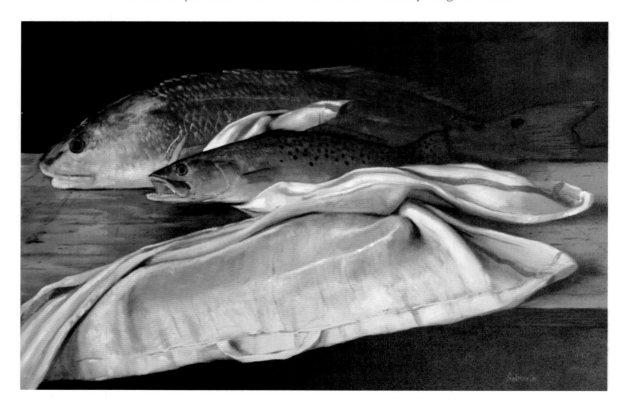

Seafood

Trout Amandine with French Fries

Recipe courtesy of Elizabeth Charbonnet
Yield: 4 to 6 servings

This is a multilevel dish, and while it is quite delicious, the key is to time the trout filets coming out of the oven while the fries and amandine sauce are still fresh.

Amandine Sauce
½ tablespoon cornstarch
2 ounces half-and-half
8 tablespoons butter
1 cup sliced almonds
1½ cups sliced mushrooms
2 tablespoons fresh parsley, chopped
2 tablespoons lemon juice
1 tablespoon Worcestershire sauce
2 sprigs fresh thyme
2 dashes of Tabasco or Crystal hot sauce
1 tablespoon white wine

French Fries
3 large Idaho potatoes
Peanut oil for frying
Kosher salt and black pepper to taste

Trout
2 cups all-purpose flour
Salt and black pepper to taste
2 eggs, beaten
¼ cup whole milk
4 cups Zatarain's Fish Fry
8 to 10 Mississippi trout filets (8 to 10 ounces each)

To make the sauce, in a small mixing bowl, whisk together the cornstarch and half-and-half and set aside. In a medium skillet over medium heat, melt the butter and add the almonds. Sauté the almonds for 2 minutes. Reduce heat to medium low, and add remaining ingredients except for the cornstarch and half-and-half mixture and wine. Sauté, stirring, for 2 minutes.

Add the cornstarch and half-and-half mixture to the pan and continue to cook, stirring, for about 3 minutes. Reduce heat to low, and drizzle the wine into the sauce. Stir periodically and add a splash of half-and-half if sauce thickens.

To make the French fries, peel and cut the potatoes into thin sticks. Rinse and then place in a large bowl of ice water for about 5 minutes. Drain on paper towels and set aside. In a pot or deep skillet, heat the peanut oil to 325 degrees. Fry the potatoes for about 1 minute. This may take several batches, depending on the size of the pot or skillet. Using tongs, remove the fries from the hot oil and place on a paper-towel-lined plate or baking tray large enough to hold the fries. Season with kosher salt and pepper. Keep warm in a 200-degree oven on an ungreased baking tray until ready to serve.

Preheat a deep fryer to 375 degrees.

To prepare the trout, place the flour, salt, and pepper in a shallow bowl. In another shallow bowl, whisk together the eggs and milk. Place the fish fry in a third shallow bowl. Working in batches, dredge the fish in the flour. Then dip into the egg wash and dredge in the fish fry. Drop the fish into the fryer and cook for 3 to 5 minutes, or until the coating is golden brown and the fish is cooked through. As the fish is done, transfer the filets to a paper-towel-lined plate.

Preheat the oven to 500 degrees.

Transfer the trout filets to a baking sheet lined with parchment paper or aluminum foil. Divide the amandine sauce among the filets and bake in the oven for 3 minutes or until the almonds are crisp and golden brown.

To serve, transfer 2 trout filets to a plate, ladle any extra sauce over the filets, and add French fries on the side. There should be a liberal amount of sauce to soak into the French fries. Repeat with the remaining filets. Serve immediately.

Chef's Note: This dish also works well as a po' boy. Simply slice French bread in half lengthwise, place a cooked filet on the bottom bread slice, slather with amandine sauce, add French fries on top, place the top bread slice on the po' boy, and enjoy.

Primo's Stuffed Trout

Recipe courtesy of Primo's Café, Ridgeland
Yield: 6-8 servings

These trout filets would be just as delicious served with a cocktail dipping sauce.

Garlic Sauce
1 egg
2 cloves garlic, minced
1 tablespoon parsley, minced
2 teaspoons ketchup
1 cup olive oil

Stuffing
4 tablespoons butter, melted
4 tablespoons all-purpose flour
1 cup whole milk
¼ cup minced green onions
¼ cup parsley, minced
Salt, black pepper, and Cajun
   seasoning to taste

½ cup minced, boiled fresh
   Mississippi shrimp
1 pint fresh Mississippi lump blue
   crabmeat, twice picked

Trout
2 cups all-purpose flour
Salt and black pepper to taste
3 eggs, beaten
2 cups whole milk
4 cups Italian breadcrumbs
8 Mississippi trout filets (8 ounces
   each)
Peanut oil for frying

To make the sauce, in the bowl of a food processor, combine the egg, garlic, parsley, and ketchup. Process for 30 seconds. While the machine is still running, slowly add the oil through the feed tube until the mixture has thickened. Transfer to a resealable container and refrigerate until ready to use. The sauce can be stored in the refrigerator for up to 1 week.

To make the stuffing, in a skillet over medium-low heat, melt the butter. When bubbling, add the flour. Stir the roux with a flat-bottomed spoon until it becomes a light blonde color. Add the milk and bring to a simmer. Add the green onions, parsley, salt, pepper, and Cajun seasoning to taste. Allow the liquid to reduce by about half. Add the shrimp and crabmeat. After about 1 minute, remove from the heat and set aside to cool.

To prepare the trout, place the flour, salt, and pepper in a shallow bowl. In another shallow bowl, whisk together the eggs and milk. Place the breadcrumbs in a third shallow bowl. If using thick trout filets, cut a pocket in them and insert the stuffing. For smaller filets, press 2 around the stuffing.

Preheat oil in a deep fryer to 375 degrees.

Season the trout with salt and pepper. Dredge in the seasoned flour and shake off the excess. Then dip into the egg wash and dredge in the Italian breadcrumbs. Carefully place into the hot oil. If using a smaller pot for frying, do this in batches. Remove when the tasty trout is golden brown. Serve immediately, drizzled with the garlic sauce.

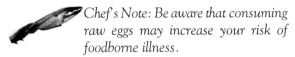 *Chef's Note: Be aware that consuming raw eggs may increase your risk of foodborne illness.*

Rustic marine wood and water colors hide everywhere in plain sight.

Anderson Family Stuffed Blackfish

Recipe courtesy of Ms. Pat Anderson
Yield: 6 to 8 servings

Stuffing
6 cups crumbled cooked cornbread
3 cups Italian breadcrumbs
3 cups whole milk
8 tablespoons butter
2 large onions, chopped
1 cup chopped celery
½ cup chopped green onions,
   including lots of green tops
3 cloves garlic, diced
3 eggs, beaten
1 teaspoon chopped fresh basil
1 teaspoon Emeril's Chicken Rub
¼ teaspoon allspice
½ teaspoon thyme
3 cups chicken stock
Salt and black pepper to taste

Sauce
8 tablespoons butter
4 tablespoons all-purpose flour
1 medium onion, minced
2 Creole tomatoes, diced
1 blackfish, cleaned and scaled
Salt and black pepper to taste

To make the stuffing, in a mixing bowl, soak the cornbread and breadcrumbs in the milk.

In a large skillet over medium-low heat, melt the butter. Add the onions, celery, green onions, and garlic. Cook, stirring, until the onions are nearly translucent, about 3 to 4 minutes.

Mix in the cornbread and bread crumbs. Add the eggs and stir. Add the seasonings, and stir in the chicken stock. If the final stuffing mixture is too dry, add butter. If it is too wet, add breadcrumbs. Cook, stirring, for another 5 minutes. Remove from the heat and set aside.

To make the sauce, in a large skillet over medium-low heat, melt the butter and then add the flour. Cook, stirring constantly, until the roux is a chocolate color. Add the onion and tomatoes and continue to cook, stirring, until the onion begins to brown. Add butter as needed to keep from drying. Remove from the heat and set aside.

Preheat the oven to 350 degrees.

Place the cleaned blackfish on a baking pan and season both sides of the fish with salt and pepper. Place the cornbread stuffing inside of the fish. Drizzle the fish with half of the sauce and reserve the rest. Tightly cover the pan with a sheet of aluminum foil and cook for 45 minutes to 1 hour or until the fish is tender and flaky.

Serve over either white or dirty rice and drizzle each serving with the reserved sauce.

Community gardens have sprung to life all along this coast, where residents are unafraid to let their artistic side shine.

Primer for Mississippi Fish Slang

The coastal accent may be difficult enough to comprehend, but then there's also the coast's slang for aquatic species offshore. The following information should help with deciphering it.

Spotted sea trout or speckled trout is otherwise known as
    Freckle fish
    Paper mouth
    Yellow mouth (large)
    Gator trout (colossal)

Red drum or redfish is otherwise known as
    Rat reds (at-limit size or under)
    Puppy drum (at-limit size or under)
    Bull reds (colossal)

Blackfish is otherwise known as
    Tripletail
    Dinosaur

Cobia is otherwise known as
    Ling
    Cobra
    Lemonfish
    Flathead
    Brownie

Mullet is otherwise known as
    Finger mullet (small)
    Popeye (average)
    Peter mullet (average)

Flounder is otherwise known as
    Flatfish
    Doormat (large)

Grouper is otherwise known as
    Copper belly
    Green eye

Sheepshead is otherwise known as
    Convict

Amberjack is otherwise known as
    Reef donkey

Dolphin is otherwise known as
    Mahimahi

Dorado is otherwise known as
    Chicken dolphin (small)

King mackerel is otherwise known as
    Snake (small)

Shark is otherwise known as
    Man in the gray suit

Redfish on the Half-Shell

Yield: 4 servings

Why are redfish always so glum?

6 fresh redfish filets, skin on
1 tablespoon extra-virgin olive oil
Salt and black pepper to taste
16 tablespoons unsalted butter
¼ cup minced garlic

½ cup white wine
Juice of 1 lemon
1 tablespoon Creole seasoning
Bonney's or Crystal hot sauce to
taste

Heat the grill to medium, about 350 degrees.

Coat the redfish filets with olive oil, dust with salt and pepper, and set aside.

In a sauté pan over medium heat, melt half of the butter, and then add the garlic. Stir until the garlic begins to brown and caramelize, but do not let it burn. Add the white wine, lemon juice, Creole seasoning, hot sauce, and remaining butter. Reduce by half and remove from the heat.

Place the filets on the grill, skin side down. Liberally coat the filets with the butter sauce and cook uncovered until the meat begins to pull away from the skin, about 5 to 8 minutes. Remove and serve.

Scranton's Red Snapper

Recipe courtesy of Richard Chenoweth, Scranton's Restaurant, Pascagoula
Yield: 4 servings

2½ cups half-and-half
¾ cup dry white wine
Juice of 2 lemons
Creole seasoning to taste
Salt and black pepper to taste
2 ounces artichoke hearts,
  quartered
2 ounces fresh mushrooms,
  quartered

1 cup all-purpose flour
2 eggs
1 box Zatarain's or other seasoned
  fish fry
Olive oil
4 6-ounce fresh Mississippi red
  snapper filets
1 pound angel-hair pasta, cooked

In reserve.

In a sauté pan over medium heat, combine 2 cups half-and-half, wine, lemon juice, Creole seasoning, salt, and pepper and bring to a simmer. Add the artichoke hearts and mushrooms and simmer for 10 minutes.

Place the flour in a shallow bowl. In another shallow bowl, whisk together the eggs and ½ cup half-and-half. Place the fish fry in a third shallow bowl.

In a sauté pan over medium-high heat, add just enough olive oil to cover the surface of the pan. Dredge the snapper filets in the flour and shake off the excess. Then dip into the egg wash and dredge in the fish fry. Transfer the filets to the sauté pan and cook until they turn golden brown on all sides, about 4 minutes per side.

To serve, place a bed of angel-hair pasta on each plate and drizzle a few spoonfuls of the cream sauce over the pasta. Place each filet over the pasta, drizzle with the remaining cream sauce, and serve.

Smoked Mullet Po' Boys

Yield: 4 po' boys

Hickory woodchips
8 fresh mullet filets, skin on
1 loaf fresh French bread
Bush's Garlic Mayo to taste (see index)

1 ripe Creole tomato, thickly sliced
1 tablespoon hot pepper jelly
1 head iceberg lettuce or bunch of arugula, coarsely chopped
1 Vidalia onion, thinly sliced

Preheat a ceramic smoker to 250 degrees. When hot, add the hickory woodchips. As soon as the chips begin to smoke, transfer the mullets to the smoker lined with aluminum foil and cook for 20 to 25 minutes. Transfer the filets to a platter, and remove and discard the skins.

Cut the French bread into –4 sections and halve lengthwise. Slather the mayo on the bottom layers of the bread, then add a layer of the Creole tomato. Add 2 filets to each po' boy and spread the filets with the pepper jelly. Add the iceberg lettuce and then the onion. Cover with the top layers of the bread and serve.

North Light Cobia

Yield: 4 to 6 servings

The North Light marks the northern end of Louisiana's Chandeleur Islands, south of Cat Island. The first lighthouse was built in 1848, and today the new North Light stands as a beacon for mariners. The area is also well known to coastal residents for its abundant cobia.

1 pound green onion sausage, sliced	1 lemon, juiced and quartered
1 red onion, diced	8 tablespoons butter
1 green bell pepper, diced	2 tablespoons prepared horseradish
4 portobello mushrooms, sliced into ¼-inch strips	2 tablespoons balsamic vinegar
4 cloves garlic, coarsely chopped	1 tablespoon Old Bay seasoning
½ bunch green onions, sliced diagonally	4-6 nice-sized fresh cobia filets
	Extra-virgin olive oil
	Salt and black pepper to taste

Preheat oven to 400 degrees.

In a cast-iron skillet over medium-high heat, cook the sausage for about 5 minutes until it starts to lightly brown. Reduce the heat, remove the sausage, and drain on a paper-towel-lined plate. Remove most of the grease from the skillet.

Increase heat to medium high and add the onion, bell pepper, and portobello mushrooms to the skillet. Cook for 5 minutes. Add the garlic and cook, stirring, for another 2 minutes. Return the sausage to the skillet, along with the remaining ingredients except for the cobia, olive oil, salt, and pepper. Mix well and reduce heat to medium low. Rub the cobia filets with olive oil, salt, and pepper. In another cast-iron skillet over medium-high heat, add 1 tablespoon olive oil. When hot, add the filets to the skillet and cook on 1 side for 15 seconds. Remove from the heat, carefully place the skillet into the oven, and broil for 5 to 6 minutes.

To serve, place a bed of white rice on a plate and pour over a generous serving of the sausage and vegetables. Place 1 cobia filet on top. Repeat with the remaining ingredients and serve immediately.

Citrus Fire Crawfish

Recipe courtesy of Terry Bounds, Moss Point
Yield: 15 to 20 servings

*Terry's crawfish are legendary on the Mississippi Coast, and he's won every cook-off he
has ever entered . . . which is actually only one.*

1 32-ounce can salt
16 ounces Chinese red pepper
16 ounces Louisiana Crab Boil
    Seasoning
16 ounces Zatarain's Pro-Boil
    Seasoning
1 8-ounce bottle Zatarain's liquid
    crab boil
1 8-ounce bottle Louisiana liquid
    crab boil

20 jalapenos, halved
2 bunches celery
5 cloves garlic, halved
1 bag new potatoes
1 pound button mushrooms
65 pounds live crawfish
1 32-ounce can pineapple juice
1 32-ounce can grapefruit juice
24 ounces lemon juice
2 bunches cilantro

In a large crawfish pot half filled with water, combine all of the ingredients
except for the live crawfish, juices, and cilantro. Bring to a boil and add
the crawfish. Return to a boil and then immediately turn off the heat. Add
the juices and cilantro and stir with a crawfish paddle. Allow to rest for 45
minutes. Remove the crawfish from the pot and serve.

 *Chef's Note: These crawfish are
so spicy that they are "on fire." To
adjust the heat, reduce the Chinese
red pepper as desired. Do a test batch
first, and then slowly adjust the spice
upwards as needed.*

*Gearing up for the obvious. With crab pots roaring to a boil
nearby, locals will automatically know what's on the menu.*

Winnie's Butterbeans and Shrimp

Recipe courtesy of Winifred Berthelot Gilbert
Yield: 10 to 12 servings

This is an old-school Mississippi Coast and South Louisiana dish pairing the perfect bean for seafood with fresh shrimp from the coast in a dark caramel-colored roux. It is ideal for gatherings of friends and family in the fall, with the first cool fronts coming through during football season.

4 quarts water
1 8-ounce bottle liquid crab boil
4 pounds jumbo (U16/20) fresh
   Mississippi shrimp
1 cup butter
1 cup all-purpose flour
2 medium onions, chopped
1 large green pepper, diced
4 stalks celery, diced
1 bunch green onions, diced

½ cup water
1 pound butterbeans or lima beans,
   fresh or frozen
Water to cover
4 bay leaves
2 teaspoons red pepper flakes
2 teaspoons thyme
2 teaspoons gumbo filé
Salt, black pepper, and Cajun
   seasoning to taste

In a large pot, bring 4 quarts water to a boil. Add the liquid crab boil. Add the shrimp and remove from the heat. Let stand for 5 minutes. Strain the shrimp and set aside to cool.

Peel and devein the cooled shrimp, and set aside in a bowl in the refrigerator.

In a large pot over low heat, melt the butter. Add the flour, increase the heat to medium low, and stir constantly with a flat-bottomed utensil to make the roux. Once the roux is a dark caramel color, add the onions, green pepper, celery, green onions, and ½ cup water, and stir. Once the onions have become translucent, add the beans and water to cover, and mix thoroughly. Add the spices. Bring to a boil. Reduce the heat to low and simmer, covered, stirring occasionally, for 1½ hours, or until the beans are soft. If necessary, add water while cooking to maintain a gravy-like consistency. Check for seasoning.

Once the beans are soft, add the shrimp and cook until the shrimp are warmed through, about 3 minutes. Remove from the heat and serve over white rice.

We start them young on the coast, and apparently they're not spicy enough for one of them.

Chef's Note: *For an added depth of flavor, crumble 5 slices cooked bacon into the butterbeans a few minutes before serving, or garnish with the bacon and a bit of chopped green onion.*

Cathead Vodka BBQ Shrimp

Recipe courtesy of Chef Kristian Wade, Stalla, Biloxi
Yield: 4 servings

Dixie Dust
2 tablespoons ranch seasoning mix
1 tablespoons iodized salt
2 tablespoons paprika
1 tablespoon black pepper
1 tablespoon onion powder
1 tablespoon sugar
1 tablespoon granulated garlic
½ tablespoon cumin
1 tablespoon chili powder

2 tablespoons chili powder
½ tablespoon granulated garlic
1 teaspoon cumin
1 tablespoon black pepper
1 tablespoon Dixie Dust

BBQ Shrimp
20 jumbo fresh Mississippi shrimp,
  peeled and deveined
4 tablespoons Dixie Dust
1 cup diced uncooked bacon
1 cup Cathead vodka
2 cups heavy cream
¼ cup BBQ Sauce
3 cups Original Grit Girl stone-ground
  yellow grits, cooked

BBQ Sauce
4 cups ketchup
¾ cup yellow mustard
½ cup honey
¾ cup apple cider vinegar

In a mixing bowl, whisk all of the Dixie Dust spices together until incorporated. Cover and store in a cool, dry area.

In a medium saucepot, mix all of the BBQ Sauce ingredients and bring to a boil. Cool and store chilled for up to 2 weeks.

Season shrimp with Dixie Dust. Place in a hot skillet and sauté on both sides until caramelized. Remove from pan and set aside. Add bacon to the skillet and reduce heat to medium. Cook until the fat has rendered out and it is crispy. Add the Cathead vodka to the pan and reduce until almost dry. Add the heavy cream and reduce until it coats the back of a spoon. Finish with the BBQ Sauce and return shrimp to the pan. Simmer until shrimp are cooked through. Serve over stone-ground grits.

Shrimp Over Sweet Potato Grits

Recipe courtesy of Georgeanne Ross
Yield: 4 servings

1 large sweet potato
2 cups chicken broth
½ cup heavy cream
1 cup Original Grit Girl stone-ground
    yellow grits, uncooked
2 teaspoons Steen's molasses
1 stick unsalted butter
1 large yellow bell pepper, julienned

1 large red bell pepper, julienned
1 cup stemmed and chopped
    mushrooms
2 pounds jumbo (U16/20) fresh
    Mississippi shrimp, peeled and
    deveined
Salt and black pepper to taste

Bake the potato for 1 hour at 400 degrees. Scrape out the flesh and set aside.

In a large saucepan, combine chicken broth and cream and bring to a boil. Stir in the potato and grits. Cover, reduce the heat to medium low, and simmer for 20 minutes, stirring often to make sure the grits are not sticking to the bottom of the pan. Mix in the molasses. Remove from heat and cover.

In a sauté pan over medium heat, melt the butter. When hot, add the peppers and mushrooms and cook until the vegetables are tender, about 8 minutes. Add the shrimp and cook for 2 minutes. Season with salt and pepper to taste. Serve the shrimp over the grits.

Shrimp au Gratin Over Grits

Yield: 10 to 12 servings

2 cups chicken broth
½ cup heavy cream
1 cup Original Grit Girl stone-ground
   yellow grits
3 cups grated Mississippi State
   University cheddar cheese
8 tablespoons butter
1 cup diced onion
½ cup all-purpose flour

1 to 2 cans evaporated milk
2 egg yolks, beaten
1 teaspoon salt
⅛ teaspoon cayenne pepper
¼ teaspoon black pepper
3 pounds jumbo (U16/20) fresh
   Mississippi shrimp, boiled,
   peeled, and deveined

Preheat the oven to 350 degrees.

In a large saucepan, combine chicken broth and cream and bring to a boil. Stir in grits. Cover, reduce heat, and simmer for 20 minutes. Stir often. Add 2 cups grated cheese and stir until melted. Remove from heat and cover.

In a skillet over medium heat, melt the butter. Add the onion and cook until translucent, about 3 to 4 minutes. Add the flour, milk, egg yolks, salt, cayenne, and pepper and stir until the sauce thickens. Place shrimp in a baking dish, cover with the sauce, and top with the remaining grated cheese.

Bake for 25 minutes or until the top is golden brown and bubbly.

Serve over grits.

Garlic Shrimp Spaghetti

Recipe courtesy of Ms. Mendy Mayfield
Yield: 6 to 8 servings

1 pound spaghetti, uncooked
4 tablespoons butter
½ cup extra-virgin olive oil
1 bunch green onions, white parts
   only, chopped
1 tablespoon garlic powder
2 teaspoons oregano
2 teaspoons red pepper flakes
2 teaspoons paprika
1 teaspoon thyme

Salt and black pepper to taste
1 head garlic, minced
1 tablespoon parsley, chopped
2 pounds jumbo (U16/20) fresh
   Mississippi shrimp, peeled and
   deveined
¼ cup white wine
½ cup freshly grated parmesan
   cheese

Boil the spaghetti according to the package directions. Strain in a colander and set aside in a large bowl under aluminum foil or a kitchen towel to keep warm. In a large skillet over medium heat, add the butter and olive oil. When the butter is melted, add the green onions and stir. When the green onions become translucent, about 3 minutes, reduce the heat to medium low and add the garlic powder, oregano, red pepper, paprika, thyme, salt, pepper, and half of the minced garlic and stir. When the garlic becomes fragrant, about 30 seconds, increase the heat to medium and add the parsley, shrimp, white wine, and remaining minced garlic. Stir. Allow the shrimp to cook for no more than 3 minutes while periodically stirring.

When the sauce is done, remove it from the heat and carefully pour over the spaghetti. Using tongs, mix the shrimp and garlic liquor thoroughly with the spaghetti. Serve immediately, dusted with the parmesan, along with a green salad and crusty French bread.

Shrimp-Stuffed Mirlitons Topped with Blue Crab

Yield: 6 to 8 servings

Stuffed mirlitons freeze well before baking. Simply wrap each in aluminum foil and place in freezer bags for later use. Also, in lieu of the crabmeat, you may simply add a pat of butter on top of the breadcrumbs before baking.

4 large mirlitons, halved lengthwise and seeded
10 tablespoons butter
1 large onion, chopped
1 green bell pepper, chopped
3 stalks celery, diced
2 bay leaves
1 tablespoon fresh parsley, chopped
6 cloves garlic, minced
5 slices bacon, cooked and crumbled

2 cups crumbled stale French bread
1 teaspoon thyme
1 teaspoon cayenne pepper
Salt and black pepper to taste
1 pound jumbo (U16/20) fresh Mississippi shrimp, peeled and deveined
½ cup Italian breadcrumbs
½ pint fresh Mississippi lump blue crabmeat, twice picked

Preheat the oven to 350 degrees.

Bring a large pot of water to a boil and add the mirlitons. Reduce heat and simmer for 20 minutes or until tender. Remove from heat and set aside to cool. Once cool enough to handle, scoop out the mirliton pulp from each half with a spoon and set aside. Be sure to leave enough pulp with the skin to form a sturdy "bowl." In a separate mixing bowl, mash the pulp.

In a large skillet over medium heat, melt 8 tablespoons butter. Add the onion, bell pepper, celery, and bay leaves and cook until the onions are nearly translucent, about 3 to 4 minutes. Stir in the mashed mirliton, parsley, garlic, bacon, crumbled bread, and spices. Mix well and cook down to a fairly thick consistency. Add the shrimp and stir together for 3 to 4 minutes. Remove from heat and generously spoon the filling into the mirliton "bowls." Transfer the stuffed mirlitons to a large casserole dish. Sprinkle the tops of each with a generous coating of the Italian breadcrumbs. Cook for 20 to 30 minutes. Five minutes before removing the mirlitons from the oven, in a cast-iron skillet over medium heat, melt 2 tablespoons butter. Stir in the crabmeat. Stir for 2 minutes and then remove from heat. Remove the mirlitons from the oven, place a heaping spoonful of the crabmeat sauce on top of each, and return to the oven. Bake for another 4 minutes. Serve immediately.

Many of the same families have fished the Mississippi Sound for shrimp and blue crab for generations, and the technology has not changed much.

John Roy's Shrimp Creole

Recipe courtesy of Jonathan C. Roy, Off the Hook, Pascagoula
Yield: 6 to 8 servings

Shellfish Stock
2 pounds jumbo (U16/20) fresh
   Mississippi shrimp
1¾ quarts water
1 onion, quartered
5 stalks celery, coarsely chopped
1 green bell pepper, coarsely
   chopped
2 teaspoons salt
2 teaspoons black pepper
1 teaspoon Cajun seasoning

Creole Sauce
¾ cup peanut oil
¾ cup all-purpose flour

1 cup chopped onions
1 cup chopped celery
1 cup chopped green bell pepper
4 tablespoons diced garlic
3 cups crushed ripe tomatoes
1½ quarts shellfish stock
½ teaspoon paprika
1 teaspoon thyme
2 bay leaves
Pinch of cayenne pepper
Salt and black pepper to taste
Few dashes of Tabasco or Crystal
   hot sauce
1 cup chopped green onions
½ cup fresh parsley, chopped

To make the stock, peel and devein the shrimp. Reserve the heads and shells and set the shrimp aside. In a stockpot, bring the water to a boil. Add the heads, shells, and remaining stock ingredients. Allow to boil for 45 minutes. Remove from the heat and strain, discarding the solids. Reserve the liquid.

To make the sauce, in a large cast-iron skillet over medium-low heat, combine the oil and flour. Cook, stirring constantly, to make a peanut-butter-colored roux. Add the onions, celery, bell peppers, and garlic. Cook, stirring, for 5 minutes or until the vegetables are wilted. Add the crushed tomatoes and stir well.

Begin adding the shellfish stock a little at a time, stirring constantly, until it has reached a sauce-like consistency. Add the seasonings. Continue to cook for 15 minutes. If the mixture becomes too thick, add a bit more stock. Add the shrimp, green onions, and parsley, and cook for another 5 minutes.

To serve, spoon the Shrimp Creole into a bowl, then place an ice-cream scoop of cooked rice on top.

Evangeline's Stuffed Crabs

Recipe courtesy of the Martin Family
Yield: About 20 stuffed crabs

16 tablespoons butter
¼ cup fresh parsley, diced
½ cup minced green onions
¾ cup minced onions
¼ cup minced celery
2 pounds fresh Mississippi lump
    blue crabmeat, twice picked
2 pounds fresh Mississippi claw blue
    crabmeat
1 cup crumbled stale French bread

½ cup whole milk
2 tablespoons Worcestershire sauce
1 teaspoon black pepper
Tabasco or Crystal hot sauce to
    taste
3 eggs
1 cup all-purpose flour
Salt and black pepper to taste
Splash of half-and-half
Zatarain's Fish Fry

In a large skillet over medium heat, melt 8 tablespoons butter. Add the vegetables and cook for 4 to 5 minutes or until the onions are translucent. Transfer to a large mixing bowl. Add the crumbled bread, milk, Worcestershire, 1 teaspoon pepper, hot sauce, and 1 egg, and mix well.

Form the mixture into patties the shape of a blue crab shell. Add more crumbled bread if too sticky. Set aside.

Place the flour, salt, and pepper in a shallow bowl. In another shallow bowl, whisk together 2 eggs and the half-and-half. Place the fish fry in a third shallow bowl.

In a skillet over medium-high medium heat, melt the remaining butter. Dredge the stuffed crabs in the flour and shake off the excess. Then dip into the egg wash and dredge in the fish fry. Working in batches, carefully transfer the stuffed crabs to the skillet and cook until golden brown, about 2 to 3 minutes. Using a spatula, flip the crabs over and continue to cook on the other side. Transfer to a platter for serving.

Primo's Eggplant Eloise

Recipe courtesy of Primo's Café, Ridgeland
Yield: 6 servings

Choron sauce is a cross between a béarnaise and tomato sauce and delicious as a savory topping for many seafood and meat dishes.

Eggplant
4 quarts water
6 ounces liquid crab boil
2 pounds jumbo (U16/20) fresh
   Mississippi shrimp
2 large eggplants
4 tablespoons butter
2 cloves garlic, minced
1 onion, minced
2 carrots, peeled and minced
4 stalks celery, minced
½ cup parsley, chopped
1 pint fresh Mississippi lump blue
   crabmeat, twice picked
Peanut oil for frying
6 cups all-purpose flour
Salt, black pepper, and Creole
   seasoning to taste
3 eggs, beaten
2 cups whole milk

4 cups Italian breadcrumbs
2 cups Choron Sauce

Choron Sauce
2 tablespoons extra-virgin olive oil
2 teaspoons minced garlic
¾ cup chopped onion
1 8-ounce can tomato paste
1 cup red wine
2 links uncooked Italian sausage,
   sliced
2 egg yolks
2 tablespoons white wine vinegar
3 tablespoons heavy cream
Dash of cayenne pepper
8 tablespoons sweet butter, melted
1 teaspoon lemon juice
1 tablespoon fresh tarragon, minced
2 teaspoons minced green onion
1 tablespoon fresh parsley, minced

To prepare the eggplant portion of the dish, in a large saucepot, bring the water to a boil. Add the liquid crab boil. Add the shrimp and remove from heat. Let stand for 5 minutes. Drain the shrimp and allow to cool before peeling and deveining. Set aside.

Peel eggplants and cut lengthwise into 1½-inch-thick slices. Hollow the top of each slice out to make a "pirogue" or boat while leaving enough eggplant to keep the structure sturdy. Set aside the eggplant that has been scooped out.

In a sauté pan over medium-low heat, melt the butter. Add the garlic, onion, carrots, celery, and parsley and cook until the onions are translucent, about 5 to 7 minutes. Add the eggplant pulp that was set aside and continue to cook for 3 minutes longer. Add the peeled shrimp. Reduce the heat to low. Add the crabmeat and mix thoroughly, cooking for 1 or 2 minutes until the shrimp and crabmeat are warm.

Preheat oil in a deep fryer to 375 degrees.

Place the flour, salt, pepper, and Creole seasoning in a shallow bowl. In another shallow bowl, whisk together the eggs and milk. Place the breadcrumbs in a third shallow bowl.

Season the eggplant with salt and pepper. Dredge in the seasoned flour and shake off the excess. Then dip into the egg wash, ensuring that the interior of each "pirogue" becomes wet. Then dredge in the Italian breadcrumbs.

Carefully place into the hot oil. If using a smaller pot for frying, do this in batches and remove when the eggplant is golden brown, about 3 minutes. Transfer to a baking sheet and keep warm in a 200-degree oven.

To prepare the sauce, in a large saucepan over medium to medium-low heat, add the olive oil and 1 teaspoon garlic. Cook for 30 seconds and then add the onions. Cook until the onions are translucent, 3 to 4 minutes. Add the tomato paste, red wine, and sausage and stir thoroughly. Allow to simmer for 1 hour or until it reduces by half. Remove the sausage and puree the sauce.

In a double boiler over medium heat, add the yolks, vinegar, 2 tablespoons heavy cream, and cayenne. Cook, whisking, until it reaches a thick consistency. Slowly drizzle in the melted butter while stirring. Then add the remaining heavy cream, lemon juice, tarragon, green onions, parsley, and remaining garlic and mix thoroughly.

Mix the 2 sauces together in the saucepan over low heat and then set aside.

Fill the eggplant pirogues with the shrimp and crabmeat mixture. Turn the oven up to 350 degrees. Transfer the eggplant to the oven to warm through. Serve with warm Choron Sauce.

Chef's Note: A simple yet crucial mistake is often made when frying eggplant. Do not prep the eggplant too early before frying and certainly don't allow it to sit for too long between frying and serving.

Verna's Oyster Dressing

Recipe courtesy of Verna Brown Meyers
Yield: 6 to 8 servings

Oyster dressing is a tradition and subject of passionate discussion on the Northern Gulf Coast, as there are many methods and variations. The following recipe is a simple and delicious old-school version, but by no means is it meant to be definitive. However, if there is one dish to start a family feud over, it would be a great-grandmother's heirloom oyster dressing.

1 pound ground pork	2 pints fresh Mississippi oysters
½ head celery with leaves, diced	2 teaspoons cayenne pepper
2 bunches green onions, chopped	2 teaspoons thyme
1 cup fresh parsley, chopped	2 bay leaves
¼ loaf stale French bread	Salt and black pepper to taste

In a Dutch oven over medium heat, cook the pork. Add the celery and green onions, and stir. Cook, covered, for 4 to 5 minutes. Carefully remove any excess grease with a spoon. Add the parsley and stir. Reduce heat to low. Break the stale French bread into small pieces, quickly dip into the oyster liquor, and add to the mixture. Mix well and cook, covered, for 10 minutes, stirring periodically. Add the drained oysters and spices, mix, cover, and cook for 20 minutes, stirring frequently. Serve immediately or freeze for up to 3 months.

Chef's Note: Dabs of canned cranberry sauce make a wonderful topping for oyster dressing, whether it is served alone or as a side for a holiday meal. Or you can halve French bread lengthwise, hollow it out to form a boat, and fill with oyster dressing. Refrigerated and then reheated, leftover dressing served simply as a sandwich on white bread with mayonnaise is one of the true pleasures in life.

Coastal Delicacies

The coast is known for fully utilizing the bounty from her waters. Most anyone who has ever grilled a monster blackfish knows the secret of the sweet and delicate cheek meat, but only the truly old-school know how to turn the fish's carcass into blackfish jelly. Generations on the coast have long known these culinary secrets, but unfortunately it is becoming a lost cooking art—sidled up into the backwaters of time until a resurgence of interest recently.

Shrimp throats, known as "spiders," are one of the more common delicacies. On the larger, jumbo to colossal sized white shrimp, there is a bit of sweet meat that is nearly always wasted. Easily freed by placing an index finger into the head along the bottom and pushing down, this tasty nugget, when washed, spiced, breaded, and fried, is an amazing twist on shrimp meat with a unique texture and makes a perfect and delicious finger food.

The mullet is one of the rare species of fish to have a gizzard, similar to a bird. As mullets are bottom feeders, it is best to use the tasty gizzards only from mullets caught near the coastal islands, where the bottoms are sandy and not full of mud. The mullet gizzard is a small little nodule about the size of a fingernail and located behind the throat. It must be sliced open and thoroughly washed before being simply spiced, battered, and fried, similar to the shrimp "spiders."

Red snapper are highly prized along the entire Gulf Coast, but at piers from Galveston to Orange Beach, the snapper throats are simply tossed out. One group of cruisers from Pascagoula would often voyage to Destin along the ICW and arrive as the Destin charter boats were docking and the fish were cleaned. The throats on the larger snappers are filled with delicate meat between the pectoral fins and are almost always scraped off the fish stations into the water for crabs or pelicans. Florida's charter captains always found it a bit curious that these Mississippi natives would walk up the piers and ask for these discarded portions of the large snappers. That was until they tasted for themselves the snapper throats scaled, spiced, breaded, and fried.

There is obviously a theme here regarding the frying of these leftover morsels of meat, but there is a reason. They have a sweetness to them not found in the other meatier portions of the fish or shrimp, and that is accentuated by the spicy batters of the Gulf Coast. Ask anyone who's tried the thumb-sized scallop of meat above and behind a redfish's eyes.

Relax and try one of these delicacies from the Gulf Coast. Done right and with the freshest of fish, it'll be reminiscent of that first hesitation over a raw oyster. A nice Comeback Sauce and saltines will certainly help the not-so-brave on that first sampling.

This too will pass.

ON THE COAST

Hooch

Whether hidden under the front porch or in the back of a cupboard, homemade hooch has a long legacy on the coast. Using fresh seasonal fruits and sugar, Mississippians will kick up their favorite liquor and remake it into special holiday tipples or something to finish off a long day of fishing before crawling into their berth. Relatively simple to make, these recipes mainly require the ingredient of time.

The Mississippi Sound is home to a mysterious island with an interesting, alcohol-related past. In what is now known as Dog Keys Pass, between Ship and Horn islands, Dog Island periodically makes an appearance. Due to the constant and natural shifting of sand to the west along the islands, it last emerged in the 1920s, but it is known to have surfaced in 1847 and the 1890s. Geologists estimate that Dog Island builds up and lasts for approximately 14 to 18 years before vanishing again into the Mississippi Sound for up to 75 years. During Prohibition, the transient island was privately purchased and became a popular resort known as the Isle of Caprice, with a very active casino. Due to a legal fluke, it was allowed to sell alcohol. However, by 1930, the island again slipped beneath the waves. The only remnant was a wellhead that constantly streamed fresh water from over 600 feet below the surface and was frequented by many a boater, including Walter Anderson, for its famed "sweet water." The pipe rising from the water is broken off now, likely by local fishermen who anchored to the wellhead, although it's unknown exactly when that occurred. However, the "sweet water" is still out there now, hidden and continuously pumping into the Sound.

Meyer Limoncello

Yield: 12 cups

Many other varied fresh citrus zests will work with this recipe - especially good are navel oranges or Satsumas. Flavoring can be controlled by the amount of zest used. Mixing together various citrus zests will also make for a tasty cordial.

12 Meyer lemons
1 750ml bottle Everclear or other
neutral high-proof alcohol

2½ cups sugar
6 cups water

Zest the Meyer lemons with a microplane or vegetable peeler, being careful to avoid the white pith. Reserve the lemons for another use. Put the zest and alcohol in a glass jar with a tight-fitting lid. Set aside in a cool, dark place for 4 days. Once the zest turns pale and the alcohol has an orange color, strain through a fine-mesh strainer. Discard the solids.

In a medium saucepan over medium heat, combine the sugar and water. Stir until the sugar dissolves and the syrup is clear. Do not allow to boil. Remove from the heat and let cool. Then in a large bowl, combine the liquor and simple syrup. Pour the lemon-infused liqueur into clean bottles with corks or screw tops. Set aside for 2 weeks to allow the liqueur to mellow.

Prepping for a fresh batch of Meyer Limoncello that will be ready for tippling in 2 weeks.

Cherry Bounce

Yield: 12 cups

To make this a holiday gift for a relative or friend, design and print out your own label and tape it onto the bottle.

1 liter bourbon
¾ cup sugar
1 pint fresh sour or pie cherries

Transfer the bourbon from the bottle into a large container. Dry the mouth of the empty bourbon bottle and, using a funnel, slowly pour the sugar into it. Add the cherries 1 by 1 into the bourbon bottle. Using a funnel, return the bourbon to the original bottle until full. There will be excess bourbon at this point—go ahead and make a cocktail with it. Seal the bottle tightly using the original cap, and with an indelible pen, mark the date on the bottle. Place in a dark cupboard or underneath the front steps for 6 months. Periodically turn the bottle upside down to agitate the mixture, and then return it to its resting place. Drink in 6 months.

The Kenwoods' Whiskey Punch

Recipe courtesy of the Kenwood Family
Yield: About 4 liters

A legend at the already legendary Kenwood Thanksgiving parties, this punch has made its way to the shores of Bay St. Louis on South Beach, where Cliff and Jennie Kenwood have a small cottage and entertain friends and family during the summer.

Juice and pulp of 4 large lemons
1 32-ounce can pineapple juice
1 8-ounce can frozen orange juice
   concentrate

1 fifth Jack Daniel's whiskey
1 cup water
1 cup sugar
2 2-liter bottles 7-Up

In a large mixing bowl, combine the lemon juice and pulp, pineapple juice, orange juice concentrate, and whiskey and mix well. Mix the water and sugar together in a microwaveable cup and heat for 2 minutes. Remove and stir into the bowl. Fill the empty orange juice container with water and add to the bowl. Repeat 2 more times, for a total of 24 ounces of water, and then add the 7-Up. Mix well. Pour into the empty 2-liter bottles and freeze for 36 hours. To serve, partially thaw 1 or 2 containers, and add extra frozen punch as needed.

Mayhaw Rum Brandy

Yield: 8 cups

3 pints fresh mayhaws, lightly
  crushed
8 cups sugar
1 750ml bottle amber rum

Thoroughly clean a ½-gallon glass jar. Coat the mayhaws in the sugar and place in the jar. Add the remaining sugar. Top off the jar with the rum, stir, and seal tightly. Place in a dark cupboard or underneath the front steps for at least 2 months. Periodically turn the jar upside down to agitate the mixture, and then return it to its resting place. Strain the liquid several times through a fine-mesh strainer until fully clear of sediment. Serve lightly chilled or at room temperature.

Peach Tickle

Yield: 12 cups

Enjoy this hooch with friends while telling fish stories. When lies are told, make them eat a peach slice from the jar.

2 pints fresh peaches, peeled and
  quartered
¾ cup sugar
1 750ml bottle rum

Thoroughly clean 4 medium Mason jars. Coat the peach quarters in the sugar and divide among the Mason jars. Fully top off each of the Mason jars with the rum and seal tightly. Place in a dark cupboard or underneath the front steps for at least 1 week. Periodically turn each jar upside down to agitate the mixture, and then return it to its resting place. Chill or sip out of the Mason jar.

Southern Light Blonde Ale

Recipe courtesy of Sam Vasquez, Mississippi Brewing Company & Gumbo House, Gulfport
Yield: 50 12-ounce bottles

Cousins Samson and Alex Vasquez started Mississippi Brewing as the demand for their homebrew grew beyond what their stovetop could produce. They opened their doors in 2013 in beautiful downtown Gulfport, creating a place for beer lovers by beer lovers. As demand grew again, they took the next step and starting bottling their two bestselling beers, Southern Light Blonde Ale and Courage Pale Ale. The following is their homebrew recipe for their top-selling coastal brew.

2½ gallons water
6 pounds Pilsen malt extract syrup
1 ounce Cascade hops
2 gallons cold sanitized water

1 pack brewer's yeast
⅔ cup priming sugar
2 cups water

First open and sip your favorite brew. Now you are ready to start.

Bring 2½ gallons water to a boil. Remove from the heat. Stir in the Pilsen malt syrup. Return the water to a boil. This mixture is now called "wort"—the term for unfermented beer. Add the Cascade hops and boil for 1 hour. Remove from the heat and cool rapidly to 100 degrees by placing the pot in an ice bath in the sink.

Sanitize and fill a primary fermenter with 2 gallons cold sanitized water. Then pour in the cooled wort. Be sure to leave the sludge in the bottom of the pot. If necessary, add more sanitized cold water to bring the volume to 5 gallons. Aerate the wort by rocking the fermenter back and forth several times, allowing it to splash. Once the temperature of the wort is between 70 and 78 degrees, use scissors to cut off a corner of the yeast pack and pour the yeast into the fermenter. Insert the airlock into the rubber stopper or lid, and seal the fermenter. Move the fermenter to a warm, dark, quiet spot until fermentation begins. Active fermentation begins around 48 hours after brewing and can be identified by a layer of foam on the surface and bubbles coming from the airlock. Active fermentation ends about 1 or 2 weeks after brewing, when the foam falls back into the beer and activity in the airlock slows or stops.

To bottle, sanitize a siphon and all other bottling equipment, including the bottles. Add priming sugar to 2 cups water and bring to a boil. Pour into the bottling bucket. Siphon beer into the bottling bucket and stir gently to mix with the priming solution. Fill and cap the bottles. After bottling, allow the bottles to rest at room temperature for 2 weeks. After this point, the bottles can be stored cool or cold.

This blue dinghy is likely no longer beached near the ranger station on the Gulf side of Horn Island, due to the constant shifting of the sands in the waves.

Chef's Note: Homebrewing is a delicate art and it is important to follow the necessary and strict procedures in brewing beer. Novices should first take a homebrewing class or learn from a seasoned pro.

The Lightship Race

For any coastal state with a large maritime community, the beauty and lifestyle on the water comes with a price. The Mississippi Coast has her scars, as several regions do, but with some paying a bit more than others over time. While hurricanes can redefine a region and the oil spill was criminal, it's important to remember that the seas can always exact their fair share seemingly on a whim—which happened in April 1983, as boaters from all walks of life stepped onboard for what they thought would be a fast and beautiful adventure out into the Mississippi Sound and Gulf of Mexico.

Hjalmer Breit, legendary sailor and eventual commodore of the Southern Yacht Club of New Orleans, was onboard *Big H*, a Charley Morgan-designed Heritage One Ton racing in the deadly Lightship Race that year.

"Next thing I know," he recalls, "I'm disoriented and on my back on the cabin floor in salt and bilge water. I look up and Harvey has got his front teeth knocked out and I scramble out on deck and see in the lightning that we're close to a breaker line, but worse—there's no one in the cockpit. I thought . . . hell of a situation."

Only 6 boats would finish the race out of the 38 that started, and no one would dispute that the U.S. Coast Guard had earned their pay that weekend. Once part of the Gulf Ocean Racing Circuit (GORC), the 180-mile Lightship Race ran a triangular ocean course outside the protection of the barrier islands of Louisiana, Mississippi, and Alabama. These islands mark the rapid rise of the seafloor from deepwater to less than 12 feet. Late April, before the Gulf Coast's hot summer doldrums, is an ideal weather window, but cool high-pressure systems diving south and colliding with warm Gulf moisture can wreak atmospheric havoc, including serious sustained winds. However, predictions were reasonable that weekend, with nothing higher than 25 knots.

The 38-boat Performance Handicap Racing Fleet handicap start was in a strong and building southerly with heavily overcast and threatening skies, and only a few boats opted to stay in the marinas. Conditions worsened during the race as a cold

(Photographs by Topper Thompson)

160

front approached from the north. Several boats had serious issues in the first few miles and didn't make it past the mark at Ship Island Pass, let alone into the open waters of the Gulf.

Guy Brierre, who crewed with Breit on the Heritage One Ton, describes the first few hours of conditions, when some of the boats were in survival mode before the first mark. "It was a shallow beat to the Ship Island Pass and we started with a #2 jib. Almost immediately we went to a #3 and by the time we hit the pass we were going to a #4, and then we reefed the main. Remember, many of these were old, heavy boats."

These were still the days of Gulf Coast sailing legends such as Tommy Dreyfus and Buddy Friedrichs and when LORAN and dead reckoning were king. Crews were spoiled if they had enough water or dry crackers onboard, let alone life jackets. But even on many of these heavy-displacement boats, with winds reported from nearby offshore oil rigs approaching sustained 40 knots—with gusts as high as 65 and seas over 15 feet—it was too much, and catastrophes started occurring on the water.

Several hours into the race and nearing the first mark, a C&C 40 had a small electrical fire and lost most of her electronics. A Hobie 33 lost her port spreader, and both immediately retired from the race. Upon docking in the Gulfport marina, their crews were not surprised to hear that several other boats had already returned or were motoring back to New Orleans through the protected MRGO Channel without their masts. A crewmember on the retired C&C recalls, "I crashed in Gulfport that afternoon and by early the next morning, I remember the hotel was shaking. I went to check it out and the wind was easily howling at over 60 knots out of the southeast. I left and went over to the yacht club and joined everyone quietly listening to the mayday calls and the efforts by the Coast Guard to rescue them."

The majority of the fleet was offshore and now rolling in the steadily worsening conditions, and by the next afternoon, the weather had truly turned. Many of the smaller boats still in the race, such as a J29 and a S2 7.9, were surfing around the course at 15-plus knots with a blade and no main. By all accounts, turning past the Mobile Sea Buoy and heading back to the west is when everything really started to hit the fan. The combination of the cold front with its 50-plus-knot sustained winds and the shallower waters near the Gulf Islands was creating an irresistible formula for disaster.

Unaware at the time that behind him a 34-foot Ericson's keel was separating

from the hull and had to be bailed continuously, or that Breit's Heritage One Ton was ahead of him in similar trouble, Topper Thompson on *Slot Machine*, a Lindenberg 30 custom light displacement, states, "After rounding the Mobile Bay sea buoy, it was deemed safest to just get home to Gulfport offshore rather than dropping out and risking threading it through one of the shallow narrow passes in the islands."

Almost all of the remaining boats in the race opted for that "safe" decision, and that led them into the really bad conditions around Petit Bois Island. On *Slot Machine*, most of the crew was puking below as they now pounded through the still chilly Gulf water under maximum reef on the main and a storm jib, with every fourth or fifth wave completely pooping the cockpit. Thompson continues, "I would like to say that we were great seamen and all of that, but most of us puked around the course and just did the work that we had to do to try and get back."

At the shallowing waters along the southern shores of the barrier islands, the erratic rollers were forced higher and higher. Brierre, onboard the Heritage One Ton, describes the harrowing last minutes when *Big H* was cratering down in troughs between the waves, so that to see the sky you had to look straight up. "Our forestay tang sheered with a loud bang and the only thing holding the mast forward was a baby stay and the jib luff. We quickly ran halyards forward to the surviving jib-tack horns and cinched them tight, saving the mast. No longer able to sail, we began motoring north, with huge help from the now-following seas to try to find the pass and put in at Pascagoula. It was the middle of the night now, and you couldn't see a thing, but you could hear each wave as it approached like a freight train. I went below off shift and it's amazing how attuned and accurate yours ears become at moments like this. We heard the next wave coming. Instead of it being behind us, it was above us. The wave broke over the first set of spreaders and the boat pitchpoled into a fully inverted position."

Thompson, onboard *Slot Machine*, explains their eventual forced removal from the regatta and their mayday calls. "Rogue waves started coming in earnest. On top of the 12-foot seas running at the time, occasional monsters would come through and break on top. It was one of these waves in particular that came through and seems to have been the harbinger of disaster. The wave broke and flipped her, stern over bow. In the same motion, the rudder was broken off. The boat came up, rig intact, but no steerage. A sea anchor was deployed, but it did not bring the bow into the wind. *Slot Machine* had no control and was broadside to the breaking waves. The crew got below deck, wedged themselves into place with sails, and tried to stow all potential projectiles. A mayday was put out and the Coast Guard was contacted. In the middle of communication with the Coast Guard, the boat rolled again and this time the mast hit the bottom and communication with the Coast Guard ceased."

Only a few miles away, the Heritage One Ton had righted. Breit climbed through the debris in the cabin and made his way towards the empty cockpit. As the vessel bore down on the breaking shoreline, Breit found two of the crew hanging off the stern attached by harnesses. He had an immediate choice to make. One of the crew was a 350-pound linebacker who had played for the Georgia Bulldogs, and the other, as Breit explains, "owed me money." Choosing wisely, he pulled in the average-weight man, and when two other crewmembers came from below, the four pulled the linebacker in from the water.

A few boats got lucky in the horrendous conditions and miraculously snuck through the passes between the barrier islands, but *Slot Machine* wasn't so lucky. Within the next hour, the boat started pounding on the beach of Petit Bois Island, and Thompson and his crew abandoned ship into the heavy surf. He recounts, "We were eight souls aboard *Slot Machine* during the Lightship Race. All survived the foundering, suffering some degree of hypothermia after having been exposed to rain and 42-degree temperatures on Petit Bois Island. Luckily, our watch captain at the helm during the pitchpole was harnessed to the rail and only suffered cracked ribs when he bent the stern pulpit and broke through the lifelines."

Having secured the crewmembers, Breit was amazed to discover that the Heritage One Ton's engine had kept running while inverted. They now steered *Big H* away from the breakers and were spotted by a Coast Guard helicopter. Using their searchlight and determining that the *Big H* was now in the least distress, the Coast Guard directed them to one of the passes and into the protected waters of the Sound, where the seas almost immediately dropped from 15 feet to what seemed like 1-foot waves.

Dealing with multiple mayday calls and making assessments on the fly, the Coast Guard helicopter then screamed away to search for a 19-year-old Tulane student, Nelson Roltsch, who had been washed off of a J29 along with their helmsman by a rogue wave. The J29 crew had successfully recovered the helmsman but were still trying to recover Roltsch. They were sailing into the breaking seas and headwinds with a 7½-hp overboard, which was useless and only in the water half the time.

Hours later, the crew of *Slot Machine* was rescued off of Petit Bois while planes and helicopters continuously searched for Roltsch. Tragically, he was never found. An accomplished Laser sailor, well liked and with fiery red hair, he had won an A Scow National Championship at age 16. He had entered Tulane in 1981 and had spent the summer as a charter captain, having earned his U.S. Coast Guard Captain's License at age 18. Tulane University of New Orleans continues to remember Roltsch by holding a well-attended and very competitive collegiate regatta in his name.

Reflecting on the trials so many years ago onboard *Slot Machine*, Thompson states, "As I recall, we never knew that Nelson was lost until Monday. I think

that we just trudged off of the Coast Guard boat and into the car, heading for home. I remember that I fell asleep in the bathtub. When we first heard that he had been lost, my initial response was that that could not have happened on the boat that I was on, but after thinking more carefully, it began to dawn on me that it could have happened to anyone, on any of the boats, and that it was amazing that it didn't happen more often."

Meat

Crooked Letter Venison Chili with Biloxi Krewe Onions

Yield: 10 to 12 servings

Venison Chili
4 tablespoons unsalted butter
1 medium red onion, chopped
1 medium yellow onion, chopped
1 red bell pepper, chopped
1 jalapeno, diced
¼ cup extra-virgin olive oil
3 tablespoons chili powder
2 heaping tablespoons cumin
1 tablespoon salt and black pepper
1 tablespoon sweet paprika
5 pounds ground venison
1 12-ounce can tomato puree
1 12-ounce can whole tomatoes
1 quart chicken stock
1 12-ounce bottle Crooked Letter
   beer

Biloxi Krewe Onions
4 tablespoons unsalted butter
6 medium onions, sliced
¼ cup extra-virgin olive oil
2 tablespoons Sriracha
1 tablespoon yellow mustard
1 tablespoon Creole mustard
1 tablespoon Tiger Sauce or
   Pickapeppa sauce
1 tablespoon rice wine vinegar
1 tablespoon Slap Ya Momma or
   other Creole seasoning
2 teaspoons cayenne pepper
Salt and black pepper to taste
2 12-ounce cans Chandeleur
   Freemason beer

To make the chili, in a large stockpot over medium heat, melt the butter. Add the vegetables, olive oil, and spices. Stir well and allow to cook until the onions become almost translucent, about 6 to 8 minutes. Add the ground venison and stir well until the meat browns. Add the tomatoes, half of the chicken stock, and all of the beer. Mix well and bring to a simmer. Simmer over medium heat, uncovered, for 45 minutes. Add the remaining chicken stock in increments to maintain preferred consistency.

To make the onions, in a cast-iron skillet over medium heat, melt the butter. Add the onions. Add the olive oil, Sriracha, yellow mustard, Creole mustard, Tiger Sauce, vinegar, Creole seasoning, cayenne pepper, salt, and black pepper. Deglaze with the beer as needed. Stir often and scrape the bottom of the skillet as necessary. When ready, after approximately 50 minutes, the onions should be almost unrecognizable and a dark caramelized color. Remove from the heat. Serve the chili in bowls, each garnished with a heaping spoonful of Biloxi Krewe Onions.

Always pay attention. Never walk quickly down residential streets on the coast.

Chef's Note: These onions are an indestructible dish, and the level of spiciness can be adjusted as desired. The only caution is to watch the salt levels. A good sign that the onions are ready is that your arm is tired from stirring and you have used a bit more of your beer to deglaze than you are comfortable with.

Venison Tenderloin with Mayhaw-Jelly Glaze and Roasted Golden Beets

Yield: 4 to 6 servings

1 8-ounce jar mayhaw jelly
1 pint apple cider
8 tablespoons butter
Salt and black pepper to taste
¼ cup extra-virgin olive oil
3 medium golden beets, peeled and coarsely chopped

1 large onion, coarsely chopped
1 bunch baby carrots, chopped
6 red potatoes, quartered
6 cloves garlic, chopped
2 1-pound venison tenderloins
1 to 2 tablespoons bacon fat

Preheat the oven to 375 degrees.

In a saucepot over low heat, melt the jelly. Increase the heat to medium, add the apple cider, and reduce to ½ cup. Remove from the heat. Add 4 tablespoons butter, salt, and pepper and mix thoroughly. Set aside.

In a skillet or cast-iron pot over medium-low heat, melt the remaining butter, and then add the olive oil. Add the vegetables, salt, and pepper and stir, cooking until the vegetables are just tender. Transfer the pot to the oven and roast for 20 minutes, stirring periodically. Remove from the oven and set aside.

Season the venison with salt and pepper. In a cast-iron skillet over medium-high heat, melt the bacon fat. Place the tenderloins in the skillet and brown on all sides. Spoon half of the mayhaw glaze onto the tenderloins to thoroughly coat. Transfer the skillet to the oven and cook for 4 to 5 minutes, until medium. Remove from the oven and let rest for 5 minutes.

Slice the tenderloins and serve with the remaining mayhaw glaze and the vegetables. This is delicious served over dirty rice.

Debris BBQ Beef on Pistolettes for Ship Island

Recipe courtesy of Elizabeth Charbonnet
Yield: 10-12 servings for hungry boaters

Since the late 1950s, the Charbonnet family of New Orleans would celebrate the 4th of July in Biloxi at the Broadwater Beach Hotel. With an army of five daughters and their friends setting up stakes at one of the Broadwater's cottages, it took a lot of food to placate these young women and eventually their own children. If this recipe could handle these young women, then surely it will feed your boat crew out on the islands.

4½ to 5 pounds beef chuck roast
Salt and black pepper to taste
1 large onion, chopped
2 tablespoons vinegar
2 tablespoons dark brown sugar
Juice of 1 large lemon
1 cup Heinz Chili Sauce
5 tablespoons Worcestershire sauce
1 tablespoon liquid hickory smoke
½ tablespoon Coleman's Hot English
  mustard

1 teaspoon chili powder
3 bay leaves
½ cup water
1 cup red wine
½ cup chopped celery
1 head garlic, peeled and minced
1 teaspoon garlic powder
1 tablespoon Cajun seasoning

Preheat the oven to 325 degrees. Season the roast with salt and pepper. In a large mixing bowl, combine all of the other ingredients and mix thoroughly. Transfer the roast to a Dutch oven and then pour the mixture on top. Cook for 6 hours, covered, periodically basting with the pot liquor. When the meat is tender and falling apart, remove from the oven. Once cool, transfer to a cutting board, and using 2 forks, shred the meat. Return the meat to the Dutch oven and cook in the oven, covered, for another 15 minutes. Remove and slather onto fresh pistolettes or crusty French bread with mayonnaise.

Chef's Note: If not serving immediately, transfer the meat to a resealable container and refrigerate for up to 1 week or freeze for up to 6 months. These make ideal and always-at-the-ready sandwiches onboard and are equally as tasty cold as they are reheated.

Pecan-Smoked Creole Brisket

Yield: 12 to 16 servings

Tay's BBQ was founded by Millard Taylor in Columbia, Mississippi in the 1940s and was resurrected by Chef Matthew and his brother-in-law Ramsay Taylor in 2002. Many of the original hickory-smoked recipes, including for the now-famous Tay's BBQ sauce, were discovered in a dusty box in the back of an attic. Before opening their doors, Chef did a batch of 4 possible new BBQ sauces as well as the old Tay's sauce, and the entire family did a blind tasting. The old Tay's sauce was the overall favorite. That recipe is a closely held family secret so unfortunately did not make it into this book. However, their tried-and-true barbecuing method for brisket is. Enjoy.

Tay's Sink Dust Dry Rub
2 tablespoons black pepper
2 tablespoons white pepper
2 teaspoons cayenne pepper
2 tablespoons garlic powder
1 teaspoon onion powder
2 tablespoons garlic salt
2 teaspoons Old Bay

1 teaspoon dry mustard
2 tablespoons sweet paprika
2 teaspoons brown sugar

Brisket
Pecan-wood kindling
6-to-8-pound brisket, flat end
Tay's Sink Dust Dry Rub

To make the dry rub, mix the dry spices together thoroughly. This yields a little over ⅔ cup.

Chef's Note: The following recipe is for one of my favorite brisket sandwiches. Slice 1 baguette in half lengthwise and add layers of thinly sliced brisket. Add sliced jalapenos and then smother with cheddar cheese. Drizzle Tay's BBQ sauce (or your other favorite BBQ sauce) on top and broil open-faced in the oven until the cheese has melted. Enjoy!

To cook the brisket, start the coals on the grill, and soak pecan-wood kindling in water for at least 30 minutes. Trim the brisket of most of the excess fat, leaving some for flavoring. Work the dry rub completely into the brisket, coating heavily. Let stand for at least 30 minutes. Place pecan-wood kindling on the hot coals. Place meat on the grill, fatty side up, away from the primary heat source. The brisket should be cooked using indirect heat, with the thickest side facing the heat. Maintain a temperature of 225 to 250 degrees for 3 to 5 hours. Do not turn the brisket while cooking. The brisket is done when the internal temperature reaches 165 to 170 degrees. Remove from the grill and allow to rest in a pan, covered with aluminum foil, for at least 30 minutes. To serve, remember to slice against the grain of the meat.

Eagle Point Beef Daube

Yield: 4 to 6 servings

This is a lot of beef, but the leftovers will freeze very well.

4 to 5 pounds beef chuck roast
Salt and black pepper to taste
1 cup + 1 tablespoon canola oil
1½ cups all-purpose flour
2 medium onions, diced
4 stalks celery, diced
2 medium carrots, diced
1 red bell pepper, diced
10 cloves garlic, coarsely chopped
2 jalapenos, seeded and diced
1 cup red wine

1 tablespoon balsamic vinegar
1 quart beef stock
1 35-ounce can whole tomatoes
2 15-ounce cans tomato sauce
1 6-ounce can tomato paste
2 bay leaves
1 teaspoon cayenne pepper
1 tablespoon Creole seasoning
1 tablespoon oregano
1 tablespoon thyme
1 pound spaghetti, cooked

Thoroughly season the chuck roast with salt and pepper. In a cast-iron skillet over high heat, add 1 tablespoon canola oil. Sear the chuck roast on all sides until nicely browned. Remove from the heat and set aside.

In a Dutch oven over medium heat, combine the remaining oil and the flour to make a roux. Cook, stirring constantly, until it reaches a dark chocolate color. Add the onions, celery, carrots, bell pepper, garlic, and jalapenos. Cook until the vegetables are tender. Add the red wine, balsamic vinegar, and beef stock. Bring to a simmer and cook for 2 to 3 minutes. Add all of the tomato products, bay leaves, and seasonings and mix well. Cook for another 3 to 5 minutes. Add the roast, cover, and let simmer on medium-low heat for 3 hours or until the beef is falling apart. Serve over spaghetti.

Liver and Onions Stirred in a Roux

Recipe courtesy of Winifred Berthelot
Yield: 4 to 6 servings

2 pounds fresh calf liver
Salt and black pepper to taste
2 cups all-purpose flour
8 strips bacon, cooked with
  drippings reserved

4 tablespoons butter
6 large onions, coarsely chopped
½ cup water
Cajun seasoning to taste

Season the calf liver with salt and pepper and dredge in 1½ cups flour. In a large cast-iron skillet over medium-high heat, reheat the bacon drippings. (Reserve the bacon for another use.) Brown the liver on all sides, about 2 to 3 minutes per side. Transfer the liver to a platter and set aside. Reduce the heat to medium low and add the butter to the skillet. When melted, add the onions. Cook the onions until translucent. Add ½ cup flour and stir. Add water as needed. Season with salt, pepper, and Cajun seasoning to taste. When the mixture develops a creamy, light-brown color, return the livers to the skillet and cook for another 20 minutes. Serve over cooked white rice or grits.

Bell Peppers Stuffed with Dirty Rice and Chicken Livers

Yield: 10 servings

If not a fan of chicken livers, simply remove that ingredient and double up on the ground beef, or better yet, add pork tasso, rabbit, or duck meat. Stuffed bell peppers freeze very well for later meals when wrapped tightly in aluminum foil and placed into freezer bags. However, this should be done before they are placed into the oven, and they do not need to be boiled first.

10 green bell peppers, seeded and
   halved lengthwise
1 pound chicken livers, diced
1 pound ground beef
Salt and black pepper to taste
¼ pound pork tasso
4 tablespoons butter
2 large onions, chopped
1 cup diced celery

1 bunch green onions, diced
2 tablespoons fresh parsley,
   chopped
2 cloves garlic, minced
1 teaspoon fresh thyme leaves
Cajun seasoning to taste
2 cups cooked dirty rice
5 ounces chicken stock

Bring a large pot of water to a boil. Add the peppers and boil for 2 to 3 minutes. Carefully remove with tongs and rinse with tap water. Set aside.

Season the chicken livers and ground beef with salt and pepper. In a large skillet over medium heat, brown the livers and beef. Add the tasso, mix well, and cook for another 3 to 4 minutes. Set aside. In a skillet over medium heat, melt the butter. Add the onions and cook until translucent. Add the celery and cook for another 3 minutes. Add the green onions, parsley, garlic, and seasonings and cook for 5 minutes longer. Drain the grease from the beef and chicken livers and add them to the onion mixture. Add the cooked rice and the chicken stock and cook until the rice is hot and the liquid has evaporated. The stuffing should be thick when ready. Once the stuffing is cool, generously fill each green pepper half. Place the stuffed green peppers on a baking tray or in a casserole dish. Place into a preheated 275-degree oven and cook for 25 minutes before serving.

Bell Peppers Stuffed with Dirty Rice and Chicken Livers ready for the oven.

The Governor's Crawfish Chicken and Dumplings

Recipe courtesy of Sam Vasquez, Mississippi Brewing Company & Gumbo House, Gulfport
Yield: 4 servings

Crawfish Chicken
2-pound whole chicken
1 onion, quartered
2 slices lemon
1 slice lime
1 teaspoon Boom Spice (see below)
½ teaspoon dried thyme leaves
1 bay leaf
Salt and black pepper to taste
3 cups water
1½ pounds Louisiana crawfish,
  cooked and peeled

Dumplings
2 tablespoons shortening
1 tablespoon butter-flavored
  shortening
2 cups all-purpose flour
1 teaspoon salt
¼ cup water

Boom Spice
2 tablespoons cayenne pepper
2 tablespoons paprika
2 tablespoons garlic powder
2 tablespoons salt
1 tablespoon black pepper
1 tablespoon dried oregano leaves
1 tablespoon onion powder
1 tablespoon dried thyme leaves

To cook the chicken, in a large pot, combine the chicken, onion, lemon, lime, Boom Spice, thyme, bay leaf, salt, pepper, and water. Simmer over low heat until tender, about 1 hour. Cool in the pot. Transfer the chicken to a platter or a cutteing board and remove the meat from the bones. Reserve the pot liquor. Discard the bones, skin, onion, lemon, lime, and bay leaf. Transfer the stock and chicken pieces to clean pot. Bring to a simmer over low heat.

To make the dumplings, in a mixing bowl, mix the shortening and butter-flavored shortening into the flour and salt. Mix in the water to form a soft dough. Place the dough on a floured surface and roll into a thin sheet. Using a knife, slice the dough into 1-inch-wide cubes.

Place the dumplings and crawfish in the hot chicken stock. Let simmer, uncovered, for 10 minutes. Cover and simmer for 10 more minutes. Serve hot.

Millard Taylor's Black Pepper Fried Chicken

Yield: 6 servings

This is best served wrapped in a gingham cloth in an antique wicker basket and enjoyed underneath a great oak somewhere on the coast.

2 to 3 whole chicken fryers,
   preferably fresh and not frozen
½ cup garlic powder
1 pound all-purpose flour

¾ cup black pepper
2 teaspoons cayenne pepper
Peanut oil for frying
Sea salt to taste

Wash the chickens very well and then cut into pieces: legs, wings, thighs, and breasts. Wash again and let drain for 2 minutes. Season with garlic powder. Mix the flour, black, and cayenne pepper together in a large resealable bag. Place the chicken in the bag and shake thoroughly to coat the pieces in the flour. Remove the chicken pieces from the bag and, working in small batches, deep fry in peanut oil at 350 degrees until the chicken is golden brown or reaches an internal temperature of 165 degrees, about 12 to 15 minutes. Transfer to a paper-towel-lined platter, sprinkle with sea salt, and serve either hot or cold.

The Pass Pork Roast

Recipe courtesy of the Charbonnet Family
Yield: 18 servings

New Orleanians have a long history of connection to the coast, with many maintaining second residences and eventually retiring there. Since the 1980s, the large Charbonnet family has celebrated holidays in Pass Christian out at Sandy Hook, and this recipe is their perfected traditional Christmas dish served alongside turkey and oyster dressing.

2 4-pound center-cut boneless pork
   loins
1 teaspoon salt
2 teaspoons black pepper
⅓ cup all-purpose flour
2 tablespoons extra-virgin olive oil
4 large sweet potatoes, peeled and
   sliced ½ inch thick

1 12-ounce package medium pitted
   prunes
2 6-ounce packages dried apricots
1½ cups Madeira wine
2 cups chicken stock

Preheat the oven to 375 degrees.

Season the pork loins with salt and pepper and dredge in the flour. In a large cast-iron skillet, heat the oil over medium heat. Add the loins, 1 at a time, and brown on all sides. Remove and place in a large lightly greased roasting pan. Arrange sweet potatoes and prunes around the pork and set aside.

Mix the apricots, wine, and stock in a large saucepan and bring to a boil. Reduce the heat and simmer for 5 minutes. Remove from the heat and pour the mixture over the pork, sweet potatoes, and prunes in the roasting pan. Tightly cover with aluminum foil (even if you use a Dutch oven with a lid) and roast for 1 hour, basting every 15 minutes.

Remove from the oven and let stand for at least 10 minutes before slicing. The sauce will have turned rich and almost black and should be generously drizzled on top for presentation. Serve over white rice with the sweet potatoes.

Cream Soda Ham

Yield: 10 to 12 servings

Leftovers from this ham make for great sandwiches.

5 cups Barq's cream soda
½ jar mayhaw jelly
½ jar hot pepper jelly
1 tablespoon Pickapeppa sauce
Juice of ½ Meyer lemon
1½ cups brown sugar

1 7-to-8-pound ham
1 stick cinnamon, ground
10 cloves, ground
Salt and black pepper to taste
1 heaping tablespoon prepared
  horseradish

Preheat the oven to 350 degrees. In a large saucepot over medium heat, bring the cream soda to a simmer. Add the mayhaw and hot pepper jelly and stir. Add the Pickapeppa, lemon juice, and ½ cup brown sugar to the syrup mixture. Reduce until it reaches a light syrupy consistency. Place the ham in the center of a large Dutch oven, and score the ham in uniform slices about ½ inch deep. Generously ladle the cream soda syrup onto the ham. Rub the remaining brown sugar, the remaining dry spices, and the horseradish onto the entire ham, ensuring that plenty make their way into the scored cuts. Lightly cover the ham with aluminum foil; this does not have to be secured and is simply to prevent scorching. Transfer to the oven and baste every 15 minutes with the syrup. Cook for 2½ to 3 hours. Once cool, slice and serve.

Ham's Almost Gone Pasta

Yield: 8 to 10 servings

1 pound rigatoni pasta
1 tablespoon extra-virgin olive oil
2 tablespoons pine nuts
2 cups diced red onions
1 large head garlic, coarsely
   chopped
¼ cup sundried tomatoes, julienned
1 bunch green onions, thinly sliced
¼ cup sweet pickles, diced
8 tablespoons unsalted butter

Juice of 1 lemon
1½ pounds ham, coarsely chopped
2 tablespoons Creole mustard
¼ cup pickle juice
1 teaspoon red pepper flakes
Salt and black pepper to taste
½ cup shredded parmesan cheese
½ cup cooked, crumbled apple-
   smoked bacon for garnish

Chef investing fresh parmesan into his cast-iron recipe.

Prepare the pasta according to the package instructions, drain, and set aside to cool. Preheat the oven to 400 degrees. In a large cast-iron skillet over medium-high heat, combine the olive oil and pine nuts and cook for 1 minute. Add the onions and garlic and lower the heat to medium. Add the tomatoes, green onions, and pickles, and cook for 3 to 5 minutes. Add the butter and lemon juice and whisk well, until the butter has melted. Add the ham, Creole mustard, pickle juice, and spices. Lower the heat to medium low and mix well in the skillet. Remove from the heat and fold in the pasta. Cover with the shredded parmesan cheese and sprinkle the bacon on top. Place into the oven, cook for 20 to 25 minutes, and serve hot.

The Coast's Second Boating Season

As the first cool fronts make their way down from the north in the late fall, and with the holidays right around the corner, the second major boating season kicks in on the Mississippi Coast. Flatboats and pirogues are readied, and marsh ponds in the flyways are scouted for mallards and teal migrating south. Fishermen head out for those big reds and trout that got away over the summer, and oystermen fan out to bring in those salty oysters so necessary for this coast's holiday celebrations.

Thanksgiving and Christmas on the Gulf Coast have always featured time-honored traditions incorporating boating and holiday meals that reach back to subsistence fishing and hunting. It's hard not to notice the flatboats covered in fresh marsh grass on Thanksgiving morning in Diamondhead, with hunters in their camouflage gear rushing to get the smokers started. At the boat launches along the coast, boats skippered by "paw paws" are eased back onto their trailers, the proud grandkids ready for a nap after trawling shrimp for the gumbo pots. In Bay St. Louis, crab traps are raised and early-morning trout are cleaned, while the luggers in Pass Christian bring in those all-important oysters.

As families descend on their gathering spots on the coast from Pass Christian to Moss Point and from Pearlington to Ocean Springs, the kitchens and the "men's" kitchens out back come alive. Recipes handed down from generations long past are taught to the next in line. The number of oysters in this year's dressing is marked on the handwritten recipe that now scrolls back 50 years. Empty shotgun-shell casings and old tangled fishing lines are placed amongst moss, green mirlitons, and heirloom crystal candleholders for table centerpieces, while the smell of redfish and etouffees and the sound of laughter permeate the houses. Out back, brothers and uncles sip on cold beer and their sons and daughters watch as mallards wrapped in bacon and dusted with brown sugar are smoked to perfection—the hopeful black labs at their heels waiting for just that one dropped bird—just one, please.

On piers and docks behind the houses, oysters are charbroiled while the brisk winds whip down across the sounds and bays and the boats pop in the water, the sailboat stanchions clinking. The windows of the homes beam with warm light, and the trucks of the gathered families and friends are parked on the lawn under sprawling oaks beside a few boat trailers with license plates hailing from the counties of Hancock, Harrison, and Jackson—all still wet from pulling in their launches.

Out at Eagle Point in Ocean Springs, if someone arrives with a sack of oysters, the grills heat up and inevitably lead to impromptu pier parties. Marathon charbroiling of the rocks continues until past sunset.

For many boaters across the country, the arriving winter means putting their boats to bed under cover for the inevitable snow and ice. On the Mississippi Coast and throughout the Gulf South, however, boating springs to life in a second season. Away from the summer waterskiing, regattas, and waiting in the heat for that tuna to bite offshore, many might say that it's the more important boating season.

Desserts

Never-Fail Piecrust

Yield: 1 9-inch piecrust

1½ cups shortening
3 cups all-purpose flour
1 teaspoon salt

1 egg, beaten
5 tablespoons water
1 tablespoon vinegar

In a mixing bowl, using a mixing spoon, fold the shortening into the flour. Add the salt, egg, water, and vinegar and blend until smooth. Roll out and fashion into a pie shell. The dough will keep in the refrigerator for up to 2 weeks.

Walk the quiet streets along the coast, where residents wear their creativity on their sleeves, or in this case from a young oak tree.

Cornmeal Pie with Amaretto Crème Fraiche

Yields: 2 pies

This is the only time that cornmeal and sugar shall ever be allowed to meet.

Amaretto Crème Fraiche
1 cup heavy cream
2 tablespoons buttermilk
½ teaspoon amaretto

Cornmeal Pies
16 tablespoons unsalted butter,
    room temperature
1½ cups sugar

½ teaspoon vanilla extract
3 eggs
½ cup heavy cream
½ cup light corn syrup
½ cup buttermilk
3 tablespoons all-purpose flour,
    sifted
½ cup Original Grit Girl cornmeal
2 9-inch pie shells, unbaked

To make the crème fraiche, mix the cream, buttermilk, and amaretto and seal in a Mason jar. Allow to chill in the refrigerator for 8 to 24 hours to thicken.

Preheat the oven to 350 degrees. In a large mixing bowl, cream the butter with the sugar and vanilla. Add the eggs 1 at a time and whisk until the mixture comes together. Add the cream, corn syrup, and buttermilk, and whisk. Add the flour and cornmeal and whisk well. Pour into the unbaked 9-inch pie shells and bake for 30 minutes. Reduce the heat to 300 degrees and bake for another 25 minutes. Return the heat to 350 degrees and bake for another 5 minutes to allow to brown. Remove and let cool before serving. Refrigerate if not serving immediately. Serve with the Amaretto Crème Fraiche.

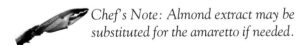

Chef's Note: Almond extract may be substituted for the amaretto if needed.

Buttermilk Pie

Yield: 1 pie

8 tablespoons unsalted butter, room temperature
1½ cups sugar
3 eggs
1 teaspoon vanilla extract
2 tablespoons all-purpose flour

1 teaspoon lemon zest
Pinch of salt
1 cup buttermilk
1 9-inch pie shell, unbaked
Nutmeg for dusting

Preheat the oven to 450 degrees. In a large mixing bowl, blend the butter with the sugar. Add the eggs and vanilla and beat until creamed together. Sift the flour into the mixture, add the lemon zest, salt, and buttermilk, and whisk well. Pour into the unbaked 9-inch pie shell and bake for 10 minutes. Reduce the heat to 325 degrees and bake for another 50 minutes or until the pie is set. Remove, let cool, and dust with nutmeg. Refrigerate if not serving immediately.

Shearwater Chess Pie

Yield: 1 pie

The Anderson family compound, known as Shearwater, overlooks the Mississippi Sound and the Ocean Springs Harbor from a magical pine-and-oak-filled bluff that was devastated by Hurricane Katrina in 2005. Family members methodically combed the grounds and marsh after the storm for family artifacts, pottery—anything. One item rediscovered was an old weathered tin holding hundreds of Anderson recipes. Intact, it scrolled back through the generations. After allowed to dry, the recipes were deciphered and rewritten by hand. The following is one of them.

2 eggs
1 tablespoon all-purpose flour
1 tablespoon cornmeal
1 teaspoon vanilla extract
¼ cup whole milk
1 cup sugar
½ cup brown sugar

4 tablespoons unsalted butter,
   melted
1 teaspoon vinegar
Pinch of salt
1 9-inch pie shell, unbaked
Confectioners' sugar for dusting

Preheat the oven to 325 degrees. In a large mixing bowl, combine the eggs, flour, cornmeal, vanilla, milk, sugars, butter, vinegar, and salt until mixed well. Pour the mixture into the unbaked 9-inch pie shell. Bake for 45 minutes. Increase the oven temperature to 350 degrees and bake for another 8 minutes. Remove and allow to cool before serving, about 30 minutes. Dust with confectioners' sugar immediately before serving, or place in a pie safe if serving to company the next day.

Chef's Note: There is no reason on earth if you are a fan of pecans to not go ahead and add a top layer of pecans to this pie. Space out the pecans evenly on top of the pie and gently push each one down into the filling before it goes into the oven.

Legendary potter Peter Anderson, focused and enjoying his art at Shearwater Pottery.

Egg Custard Pie

Yield: 1 pie

1 cup sugar	2 eggs
2 tablespoons all-purpose flour	1 cup whole milk
8 tablespoons unsalted butter, melted	1 9-inch pie shell, unbaked
	Nutmeg for dusting

Preheat the oven to 350 degrees. In a bowl, add the sugar, flour, and melted butter, and cream the mixture thoroughly. Add the eggs, 1 at a time. Add the milk and mix thoroughly. Pour into the unbaked 9-inch pie shell and bake for about 40 to 45 minutes or until the pie is set. Sprinkle with nutmeg. Chill in the refrigerator for at least 2 hours and serve.

Unlikely treasures find brief homes on the barrier islands. In a few days, a squall will send this crab-trap float on to a new destination. These islands are in a constant state of flux, but not the opportunities for beachcombing.

Caramel Pecan Pie

Yield: 1 pie

1 cup brown sugar, firmly packed
½ cup sugar
1 tablespoon all-purpose flour
8 tablespoons unsalted butter,
  melted

2 eggs, beaten
2 tablespoons whole milk
1 teaspoon vanilla extract
1 9-inch pie shell, unbaked
1 cup pecans, coarsely chopped

Preheat the oven to 325 degrees. In a bowl, add the sugars, flour, and melted butter, and cream the mixture thoroughly. Add the eggs, 1 at a time. Add the milk and mix thoroughly. Add the vanilla and mix thoroughly. Pour into the unbaked 9-inch pie shell. Sprinkle with the pecans to cover. Bake for about 45 to 50 minutes or until the pie is set. Chill in the refrigerator for at least 2 hours and serve.

Pumpkin and Pecan Pie

Yield: 1 pie

½ cup pecans, chopped
1 cup brown sugar
4 tablespoons unsalted butter,
  melted
2 eggs, beaten
1¾ cups pumpkin, blended until
  smooth

1 8-ounce can evaporated milk
½ teaspoon salt
1 teaspoon cinnamon
½ teaspoon nutmeg
½ teaspoon ginger
1 9-inch pie shell, unbaked

Preheat the oven to 425 degrees. In a mixing bowl, combine the pecans, ¼ cup brown sugar, and the butter and set aside. In a separate mixing bowl, add the eggs, the remaining brown sugar, pumpkin, milk, salt, and spices and mix well. Pour the mixture into the unbaked 9-inch pie shell. Bake for 15 minutes. Reduce the heat to 350 degrees and continue baking for another 20 minutes. Remove from the oven. Carefully arrange the pecans along the edge of the pie. Return to the oven and bake for another 10 minutes. Transfer from the oven to a cooling rack. Serve the pie warm or at room temperature.

Meyer Lemon Icebox Pie

Yield: 1 pie

5 Meyer lemons	1 9-inch pie shell, baked
2 cans condensed milk	1 cup sour cream
2 egg yolks	3 tablespoons confectioners' sugar
1 teaspoon vanilla extract	

Using a microplane or vegetable peeler, zest ½ tablespoon zest from a lemon, taking care to avoid the white pith. Set aside. Juice the lemons until you have 1 cup juice. Pour the lemon juice through a semi-fine-mesh strainer into a large bowl. Add the condensed milk, egg yolks, and vanilla, and whisk thoroughly. Pour into the baked 9-inch pie shell and then refrigerate for 2 hours.

In a separate bowl, whisk together the sour cream and confectioners' sugar. Remove the pie from the refrigerator and gently spoon the topping onto the pie. Dust the pie with the lemon zest. Return the pie to the refrigerator and chill for at least 4 hours and up to overnight.

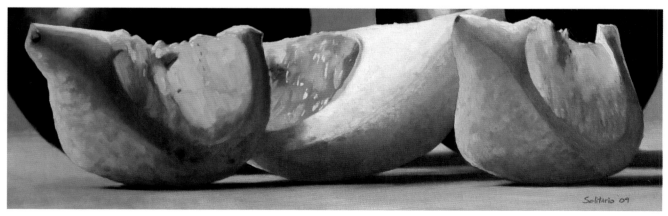

Cast-Iron Cake

Yield: 1 cake

1 cup whole milk
½ cup shortening
1½ teaspoons almond extract
2 cups all-purpose flour
1½ cups sugar

4 teaspoons baking powder
1 teaspoon salt
4 large egg whites
Confectioners' sugar for sifting

Preheat the oven to 350 degrees. In the bowl of a standing mixer or using a hand mixer, cream the milk and shortening together for about 3 minutes until it is the consistency of cottage cheese. Mix in the almond extract. In a separate bowl, add the flour, sugar, baking powder, and salt. Mix thoroughly. Add the flour mixture to the milk in 3 additions, mixing well after each addition. Add the egg whites and mix just until all the ingredients are well combined. Grease and heavily flour a 10-inch cast-iron skillet (do not use spray) and pour in the batter. Bake for 40 minutes. Test for doneness using a toothpick. Transfer from the oven to a baking rack and let cool for 45 minutes before serving. Sift confectioners' sugar on top as desired.

Bread Pudding with Whiskey Sauce

Yield: 18 servings

Bread pudding has undergone an explosion of modern variations, and some cooks have even created savory versions. This tried-and-true recipe can serve as a delicious tutorial for your own bread-pudding explorations or is indeed amazing on its own.

Bread Pudding
1 quart whole milk
2 cups sugar
1 loaf French bread, stale
3 eggs, lightly beaten
2 tablespoons vanilla extract
1 cup raisins
¼ cup coconut flakes
4 tablespoons unsalted butter, melted

Whiskey Sauce
8 tablespoons unsalted butter, melted
1 small can evaporated milk
1 cup sugar
1 egg yolk, lightly beaten
3 ounces bourbon

Bread pudding drizzled with a warm whiskey sauce.

Preheat the oven to 350 degrees.

For the bread pudding, in a large bowl, mix the milk and sugar together. Break the French bread into pieces and add to the sweet milk. Let soak for 1 hour, stirring occasionally. Add the eggs, vanilla, raisins, and coconut and stir well. Pour the melted butter into the bottom of a 9x13 baking dish, coating the sides of the dish. Pour in the pudding mixture and cover with aluminum foil. Bake for 1 hour. Uncover and continue baking for another 15 minutes or until the top is golden brown. Remove from the oven and cut into large squares.

For the whiskey sauce, in the top of a double boiler, combine the butter, evaporated milk, sugar, and egg yolk. Set the double boiler over medium heat until the water in the bottom pan begins to simmer. Stir the sauce until it thickens. Add the bourbon. Drizzle over warm squares of the bread pudding and serve.

Butterscotch Haystacks

Yield: 12 or more servings

These are more like a snack than a dessert.

1 cup butterscotch chips
½ cup peanuts
1 cup chow mein noodles

Melt the chips in a double boiler or the microwave. Add the peanuts and mix well. Add the chow mein noodles and mix, being sure to coat them thoroughly. Spoon dollops of the mixture onto wax paper and allow to harden. Serve immediately or transfer to a resealable container for up to 2 weeks.

A view of an afternoon thunderstorm passing through, from Shearwater Pottery and the Anderson family compound. After these storms build and then pass in the heat of the summer, the following silence and the smell of the rain mingling with the pines and the onshore breeze become one of those indescribable daily experiences.

Mississippi Boiled Custard

Recipe courtesy of Dr. Kenneth Holditch
Yield: 10 to 12 servings

Originally known in France as crème Anglaise, *this dessert was brought to Mississippi by English immigrants and became an immediate comfort food that has survived for over three centuries.*

3 cups whole milk
1 cup sugar
2 tablespoons all-purpose flour
⅛ teaspoon salt
4 eggs, beaten

1 cup heavy cream or evaporated milk
1 tablespoon vanilla extract
3 to 4 tablespoons good bourbon or brandy

In a pot, scald the milk and then let cool a bit. In a mixing bowl, blend the dry ingredients. Whisk the eggs into the dry ingredients. Add the scalded milk and the heavy cream or evaporated milk. In a double boiler over medium heat, cook, stirring constantly, until the mixture coats the back of a spoon. Remember that it will thicken as it cools. To be sure that the custard is smooth, beat it with an electric mixer and then strain it through a fine-mesh strainer. Once cool, mix in the vanilla and the bourbon or brandy. Refrigerate, covered, until ready to serve.

Mississippi Boiled Custard with Teacakes

Recipe courtesy of Beulah Lee Martin Smith
Yield: 20 to 30 servings

Mississippi Boiled Custard
3 eggs, separated
⅓ cup + 3 tablespoons sugar
¼ teaspoon salt
6 cups whole milk
1 teaspoon vanilla extract

Mouse's Teacakes
1½ cups sugar

16 tablespoons unsalted butter,
  room temperature
1 teaspoon vanilla extract
2 eggs, room temperature
¼ cup half-and-half
½ teaspoon freshly ground nutmeg
¼ teaspoon ground ginger
2½ cups all-purpose flour

To make the custard, in a mixing bowl, whisk the egg yolks. Slowly add ⅓ cup sugar. Add the salt and mix thoroughly. In a saucepot, scald the milk. Into a double boiler set over medium heat, pour the scalded milk. Mix in the yolks and let thicken. In another mixing bowl, beat the egg whites until stiff. Add the vanilla. Add 3 tablespoons sugar a little at a time, folding and mixing to allow the sugar to dissolve completely. Slowly fold the beaten egg-white mixture into the milk and yolks in the double boiler. Remove from the heat.

To make the teacakes, preheat the oven to 350 degrees. In a large mixing bowl, cream the sugar and butter until light and fluffy. Add the vanilla. Stir in the eggs, 1 at a time. Add the half-and-half, nutmeg, and ginger. Sift the flour and then slowly add to the mixture until it begins to hold its shape. When ready, the dough should drop off of a spoon but still retain its shape. Press into a disc, and refrigerate until firm. On a floured surface, roll the dough out to ¼-inch thickness. Cut into about 20 thin, 2-inch rectangles.

Grease a baking sheet. Place the teacakes on the sheet, about ¼ inch apart. Transfer to the oven and bake for 10 minutes or until they are golden brown. When done, remove from the baking sheet and allow to cool completely. Serve the boiled custard warm in a punchbowl or in individual ramekins, with the teacakes for dipping. The cakes can be stored in an airtight container for 3 to 4 days.

Oct 7-1992

Boiled Custard.
2 quart whole milk
3 egg yolks
3 egg whites.
3 tablespoons sugar.
⅓ cup sugar.
¼ teaspoon salt.
1 teaspoon Vanilla extract.
Scald milk over hot water,
then remove. Beat yolks well
and add ⅓ cup sugar a small
amount at a time - add salt
and salt and stir in.
add heaten yolks to milk
stirring all the time
Return mixture over hot
water (or medium heat.
and cook until thick.
Beat whites until stiff
and add 3 Tablespoons
sugar a little at a time.
folding in or heating until
well dissolved (a must)
Fold heaten whites into hot
milk mixture.
This Boiled Custard is
served @ hot in punch
Bowl or in small cups.
With cookies or fruit cake,
or what ever.
gave to RB. 40 years ago
Oct 7-1992

Lace Cookies

Yield: 15 cookies

2 cups oats
2 cups sugar
½ teaspoon salt

8 tablespoons unsalted butter, melted
2 eggs, beaten
1 tablespoon vanilla extract

Preheat the oven to 325 degrees. In a mixing bowl, mix the oatmeal, sugar, and salt well. Add the melted butter and mix well. Add the eggs and vanilla and mix until combined. Drop dollops of the dough onto a greased baking sheet. Bake for 12 minutes or until golden brown. The cookies can be stored in an airtight container for 3 to 4 days.

Beulah's Oatmeal and Pecan Cookies

Yields: 15 cookies

1 cup sugar
1 cup brown sugar
16 tablespoons unsalted butter
1 cup canola oil
2 eggs, beaten

1 teaspoon vanilla extract
3½ cups all-purpose flour
1 cup crispy rice cereal
1 cup oats
1 cup pecans, crushed

Preheat the oven to 350 degrees. In a mixing bowl, combine all the ingredients and mix thoroughly. Drop 1 tablespoon batter onto a greased baking sheet. Repeat with the remaining batter. Bake for 20 to 30 minutes. The bottoms should be brown and the tops a golden brown. Serve. The cookies can be stored in an airtight container for 3 to 4 days.

The Coastal Picket Forces

During a hot summer night in June 1942, the German submarine U-166 took aim at a U.S. Coast Guard patrol vessel that was escorting the passenger ship SS *Robert E. Lee* about 25 miles south of the mouth of the Mississippi River. Within an hour, the passenger ship would join the 56 other ships sunk off the Northern Gulf Coast during World War II. Nearly 100 lives were lost on the SS *Robert E. Lee*, and the Coast Guard escort ship would claim the only sinking of a German submarine off the Southern U.S. coastline.

In July 2014, the man who discovered the wreck of the *Titanic*, Robert Ballard, and a team of scientists aboard his exploration vessel *Nautilus* conducted an expedition to study the long-term effects of the 2010 BP Deepwater Horizon oil spill. In the process, they documented many of these stricken World War II vessels, and a lost chapter in American maritime history emerged. With the help of remotely operated underwater vehicles equipped with high-definition cameras, many of these never-before-seen wrecks, some resting more than 5,000 feet deep, finally came in from the shadows and illuminated the straits in which the United States found itself during the early stages of the war. It was a situation that sent recreational boaters, including many Mississippi shrimpers and yachtsmen, charging onto the frontlines to defend the country.

After 6 U-boats managed to sink 41 ships in the targeted waters of the East Coast and the Florida Straits, a second, larger operation codenamed Drumbeat was launched by the German navy, the Kriegsmarine, in 1942. At the time, many U.S. citizens were still ignoring the government's calls for coastal blackouts, which meant that the freighters and tankers moving along the shores at night were conveniently silhouetted for the German navy. Taking advantage of that, an armada of 22 U-boats approached the U.S. coastline and the attacks were constant.

In March 1942 alone, 70 American ships were lost to the U-boats on the U.S. East and Gulf coasts, in what the Nazis terrifyingly referred to as the "American hunting season." This ongoing attack was kept largely secret from the American people by the U.S. government, which didn't want to admit how thinly stretched and outclassed the U.S. Navy and the U.S. Coast Guard were at this stage of the war—this despite several of the tankers exploding and burning for hours in plain view of port cities and their populations.

Finally, after many of the Gulf Coast's vital fuel tankers supplying the Northeast

were sunk, the oil and gas industry informed the U.S. War Department that the burgeoning war economy would grind to a halt from a lack of fuel in only nine months. With 19 U-boats operating daily along the coastline, the U.S. government was under pressure, and at somewhat of a loss, to counter the serious threat. At the time, the U.S. Navy was ramping up the building of new warships, while the existing vessels were occupied with convoy patrols to England and Russia as well as with fending off the Japanese in the Pacific.

Immediately following the attack on Pearl Harbor, a ragtag fleet of recreational boaters, the owners of schooners and powerboats, surprisingly stepped forward and offered up their personal boats for antisubmarine operations along the American coastlines. These "Coastal Picket Forces," made up entirely of civilian volunteers, laid the groundwork for the modern-day Coast Guard Auxiliary. Through the first 18 months of the war, this volunteer group of skippers, crews, and boats only grew larger.

Ernest Hemingway and the crew onboard his 38-foot fishing boat, *Pilar*, were the most famous examples of this citizen force. He patrolled the Florida Straits in search of German U-boats while armed with only grenades and Thompson submachine guns. While Hemingway's actions certainly added to his legacy, he also gave a symbolic face to the thousands of American yachtsmen and yachtswomen volunteering their time and vessels to defend the coastline of the United States and the vital supply lines through the Gulf of Mexico and Caribbean. By August 1942, it was reported that nearly every yacht club along the Gulf and East coasts had banded together to form a flotilla. This civilian navy fleet was a true sampling of the boating traditions around the country, from yacht owners in the Northeast to shrimpers in the Gulf of Mexico.

Dedicated to new roles, the armada in Salem and Marblehead, Massachusetts, conducted 12-hour winter patrols in skiffs. In Boston, 60 sailboats and 40 powerboats actively patrolled the coast. At Cape Fear, North Carolina, the local flotilla toured the area around the clock, enduring storms and the blazing heat of summer. Off the coasts of Louisiana and Mississippi, a convoy of 126 shrimp boats had crewmembers on constant watch for submarines while continuing to bring in their hauls of Gulf shrimp.

The flotillas also became vital in rescuing seamen from torpedoed vessels, freeing up the Coast Guard to actively hunt marauding U-boats. In one instance, when a Mexican tanker lay engulfed in flames and rapidly sinking just off the beaches of Florida, hundreds of citizens watching in horror witnessed the local flotilla "drive their little boats right into the flames" to retrieve survivors.

In 1942, *Popular Science* magazine ran an article discussing this burgeoning new citizen wing of the Coast Guard, formed only months before. It stated that their "knowledge of seamanship, navigation, and gas engines, plus familiarity with local waters and boats, make a national defense asset immediately convertible to a useful purpose." It continued, "These men would be greenhorns aboard a battlewagon, but along the lines of their own hobby, many of them are extremely good, and so are their boats."

Utilizing shrimp boats, fishing vessels, luggers, and all manner of powerboats and sailboats, the Coastal Picket Forces were equipped with military radios and armed when possible. Of particular use to the U.S. Navy and Coast Guard were large offshore-racing schooners. They were naturally stealthy, fast, and equipped to handle heavier seas. These racing crews were known to patrol over 150 miles offshore. Upon spotting a U-boat, the citizen crews were asked to maintain contact as long as possible, even if this meant their "certain destruction."

In 1942, Willard Lewis and his crew were patrolling the waters off Fort Lauderdale, Florida, in his 38-foot cruiser when he had one of the more noteworthy run-ins with a German U-boat. Having been directed by the Coast Guard to search for survivors from a torpedoed tanker, he spotted a U-boat having mechanical issues with its diving fins, causing it to repeatedly resurface. Lewis radioed in the sub's position and then stated to his crew that the Coast Guard would never believe that they'd spotted a German submarine. Within minutes, though, the sub resurfaced directly underneath his cruiser, hobbling his boat and leaving telltale proof—paint smudges—on his hull.

Lewis's story was only one of many. Official historical Coast Guard documents state that "time after time, these auxiliaries took their tiny boats out, a few armed with rifles, others with only boat hooks and flashlights, to haul drowning, burned, merchant seamen from the sea."

As the *Nautilus* and Robert Ballard continued to document the wrecks nearly a mile down on the floor of the Gulf of Mexico, the video and images they produced record just how close the war came to our doorstep. The sunken ships today lie all along our coasts, serving both as thriving homes for corals, fish, and other marine species and as memorials to the actions of those able-bodied American citizens throughout World War II. By the end of the war, the Coastal Picket Forces were formally recognized and absorbed into the Coast Guard Auxiliary, which still patrols our coastlines today and operates as a "civilian arm" of the peacetime Coast Guard.

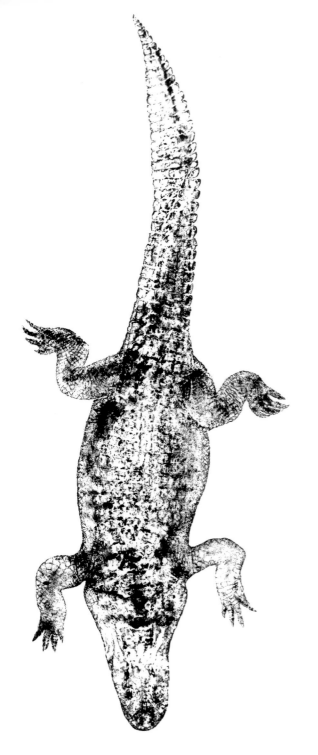

Craig Brumfield

Born and raised in Mississippi, Craig Brumfield is a fast-rising star on the coast's art scene. His mad passion for fishing and hunting and his love for everything in the wilds of the Mississippi Coast are reflected in his work. After studying art at Ole Miss, Craig worked as a fishing guide in the Chandeleur Islands for a decade. Like so many others, his life was changed by Hurricane Katrina and the BP oil spill. He became a full-time artist, working in the mediums of oil, pencil, carvings, ink, and scrimshaw, but is perhaps best known for his gyotaku works using monster billfish. Craig is a resident of and maintains a studio in Ocean Springs.

Left: At 15.9 feet and 1,011.6 pounds, this gator holds the official world record for largest alligator ever caught. Craig Brumfield used the traditional Japanese method of printing fish, or gyotaku, using ink and a full-size canvas to capture this monster in its full scale and glory. (Photograph by Craig Brumfield)

198

Sleepy fish (Tripletail) Courtbouillon

2 tsp butter
2 yellow onions
2 Bell peppers
1 Garlic clove
Salt/Pepper

Flour
Veg. oil > roux
2   8 oz. tomato paste
1   12 oz. tomato sauce
2   12 oz. diced tomato

2 Fresh tripletail fillets (18/22" size fish)
Rice

Get or catch a tripletail (sleepy fish)... filet fish and put in fridge or on ice ... In a Dutch oven or covered pot start a roux up while adding salt to taste ..... dice trinity (veggies) and add roux once chocolate color stir/mix in well on low ... add tomato sauce, paste, diced and season ... cook on med. while stirring occasionally for 15/20 min ... add 2 filets on top, put lid on cook for 15 min. on med.... cut back to low and cook .. prepare rice simmer 45 min serve over rice with french bread .. like all recipes this is the way I prepare and changes can always be made to taste ... garnish w/ lemon and green onions on top.. enjoy and eat fresh Gulf coast seafood

CraigB

Measurements

Kitchen Measures

Scant	Equals a little less than the measurement
1 black-eyed pea	⅛ teaspoon
1 tablespoon	3 teaspoons
1 fluid ounce	2 tablespoons
¼ cup	4 tablespoons
1 hen egg	About ¼ cup
⅜ cup	6 tablespoons
½ cup	8 tablespoons
1 cup (dry)	16 tablespoons
1 cup (liquid)	8 fluid ounces
1 pint	2 cups
1 quart	2 pints
1 gallon	4 quarts
1 peck	8 quart
1 peck tomatoes	15 pounds
1 bushel	4 pecks
1 pound	16 ounces
1 pound (liquid)	2 cups
1 ounce flour	4 tablespoons
1 pound flour	4 cups
1 pound sugar	2 cups
1 pound brown sugar	2⅔ cups
1 pound confectioners' sugar	3½ cups
1 ounce butter or salt	2 teaspoons
1 pound butter	2 cups
9 medium eggs	1 pound
1 ounce chocolate	¼ cup
1 ounce bitter chocolate	1 square
1 pound solid, picked crabmeat	2 cups

Measurement Abbreviations

teaspoon	tsp.
tablespoon	tbsp.
ounce	oz.
cup	c.
pint	pt.
quart	qt.
gallon	gal.
peck	pk.
bushel	bu.
pound	lb.
square	sq.

Oven Temperature Terms

Slow oven	250 to 325 degrees
Moderate oven	350 to 375 degrees
Hot oven	400 to 450 degrees
Very hot oven	450 to 500 degrees

Shrimp Count (Headless, Unpeeled)

Extra Colossal	U10
Super Colossal	U12
Colossal	U13/15
Extra Jumbo	U16/20
Extra Large	U26/30
Large	U31/35
Medium	U41/50
Small	U51/60
Extra Small	U61/70

Resources

Mississippi Stories and Photography

gulflatitudes.com

Art

Brown's Fine Art
630 Fondren Pl.
Jackson, MS 39216
601.982.4844
brownsfineart.com

Craig Brumfield Art
craigbrumfield.com

Pink Rooster Gallery
622 Washington Ave.
Ocean Springs, MS 39564
228.875.1218
pinkrooster.net

Red Bird Gallery
202 W. Ruskin Pl.
Seaside, FL 32459
850.231.3404
redbirdgalleries.com

Shearwater Pottery
102 Shearwater Dr.
Ocean Springs, MS 39564
shearwaterpottery.com

Studio Solitario
4531 Magazine St.
New Orleans, LA 70115
504.905.4175
billysolitario.com

Food

Bonney's Hot Sauce
Ocean Springs, MS 39201
patrickbonney@bellsouth.net

Cathead Distillery
422 S. Farish St.
Jackson, MS 39201
catheadvodka.com

Chandeleur Brewing Company
2711 14th St.
Gulfport, MS 39501
228.701.9985
chandeleurbrew.com

Crooked Letter Brewing Company
1805 Government St.
Ocean Springs, MS 39564
crookedletterbrewing.com

Crystal Hot Sauce
Baumerfoods.com

Delta Blues Rice
3731 Hwy. 8 E.
Ruleville, Mississippi 38771
deltabluesrice.com

Desportes Seafood
1075 Division St.
Biloxi, MS 39530
228.432.1018
desportesseafood.com

Mississippi Gulf Seafood
msseafood.com

Mississippi State University Cheese
msucheese.com

Original Grit Girl
Oxford, Mississippi
gritgirl.com

Steen's Molasses
119 N. Main Street
Abbeville, LA 70510
steenssyrup.com

Tony Chachere's Creole Seasoning
tonychachere.com

Uncle Duke's Geaux Jus
buttrub.com

Zatarain's Fish Fry
zatarains.com

Restaurants

Blow Fly Inn
1201 Washington Ave.
Gulfport, MS 39507
blow-fly-inn.com

Bozo's Grocery
2012 Ingalls Ave.
Pascagoula, MS 39567

Desportes Seafood
1075 Division St.
Biloxi, MS 39530
228.432.1018
desportesseafood.com

Government Street Grocery
1210 Government St.
Ocean Springs, MS 39564
228.818.9410

Jocelyn's Restaurant
1608 Bienville Blvd.
Ocean Springs, MS 39564
228.875.1925

Primo's Café
515 Lake Harbour Dr.
Ridgeland, MS
601.898.3600
Primoscafe.com

Rosetti's Café
895 Division St.
Biloxi, MS 39530
228.432.2146
qualityseafoodmarketbiloxims.com

Scranton's Restaurant
P.O. Box 2158
Pascagoula, MS 39569-2158
228.769.5944
scrantons.com

Sycamore House
210 Main St.
Bay St. Louis, MS 39520
thesycamorehouse.com

Tay's BBQ
Multiple locations
taysbbq.com

Trapani's
116 N. Beach Blvd.
Bay St. Louis, MS 39520
trapaniseatery.net

Vestige Restaurant
715 Washington Ave.
Ocean Springs, MS 39564
vestigerestaurant.com

Attractions
Beauvoir
2244 Beach Blvd.
Biloxi, MS 39531
beauvoir.org

Biloxi Maritime Museum
115 E. 1st St.
Biloxi, MS 39530
maritimemuseum.org

Ohr-O'Keefe Museum of Art
386 Beach Blvd.
Biloxi, MS 39530
georgeohr.org

Ship Island Excursions
1022 23rd Ave.
Gulfport, MS 39501
msshipisland.com

Walter Anderson Museum
510 Washington Ave.
Ocean Springs, MS 39564
walterandersonmuseum.com

Public Marinas
Bay St. Louis Municipal Harbor
100 Jody Compretta Dr.
Bay St. Louis, MS 39520
30°18'37.5"N 089°19'29.8"W

Biloxi Small Craft Harbor
679 Beach Blvd.
Biloxi, MS 39530
30°23'34.0"N 88°53'3.4"W

Gulfport Small Craft Harbor
1133 20th Ave.
Gulfport, MS 39501
30°21'57.8"N 89°5'9.6"W

Long Beach Harbor
720 S. Cleveland Ave.
Long Beach, MS 39560
30°20'49.7"N 89°8'35.7"W

Mary Walker Marina
3308 Mary Walker Dr.
Gautier, MS 39553
30°23'23.2"N 88°36'55.6"W

Ocean Springs Small Craft Harbor
1310 Harbor Rd.
Ocean Springs, MS 39564
30°24'14.4"N 88°49'23.4"W

Pass Christian Harbor
100 Hiern Ave.
Pass Christian, MS 39571
30°18'48.2"N 89°14'59.0"W

Point Cadet Marina
119 Beach Blvd.
Biloxi, MS 39530
30°23'22.0"N 88°51'34.1"W

Live Bait
Ocean Springs Marine Mart
1320 Harbor Rd.
Ocean Springs, MS 39564
228.875.0072
30°24'14.4"N 88°49'23.4"W

Charters
Chandeleur Boats—*Beachwater II*
Dean Gladney
beachwater2@cableone.net

Yacht Clubs
Bay-Waveland Yacht Club
Founded 1896
1 Yacht Club Dr.
Bay St. Louis, MS 39520
Bwyc.org
30°19'30"N 89°19'32"W

Founded in 1896, the Bay-Waveland Yacht Club in Bay St. Louis is home to world-class dinghy sailors, including current members of the Eagan family.

Biloxi Yacht Club
Founded 1849
408 Beach Blvd.
Biloxi, MS 39530
Biloxiyc.org
30°23'37"N 88°52'22"W

Gulfport Yacht Club at sunset.

Gulfport Yacht Club
Founded 1903
800 E. Pier Rd.
Gulfport, MS 39501
Gulfportyachtclub.org
30°21'65"N 89°05'35"W

Long Beach Yacht Club
Founded 1980
203 E. Beach Blvd.
Long Beach, MS 39560
Longbeachyachtclub.com
30°20'43"N 89°08'38"W

Ocean Springs Yacht Club
Founded 1969
100 Front Beach Dr.
Ocean Springs, MS 39564
osyc.com
30°24'36"N 88°50'27"W

The Pass Christian Harbor recently added 400 state-of-the-art slips and piers. The harbor is home to the Pass Christian Yacht Club, which traces its roots to 1849.

Pass Christian Yacht Club
Founded 1849
120 Market St.
Pass Christian, MS 39571
Pcyc-gya.org
30°18'40"N 89°14'43"W

Singing River Yacht Club
Founded 1970
3900 Beach Blvd.
Pascagoula, MS 39567
Singingryc.com
30°20'24"N 88°31'18"W

While maybe not properly positioned to get your bearings, the sentiment is nevertheless correct.

About the Authors

A native of New Orleans, Troy Gilbert grew up visiting the Mississippi Coast on weekends and eventually attended St. Stanislaus College in Bay St. Louis. As an adult, he began sailing the coast and exploring the Gulf Islands and has written about these waters for publications such as *Sailing World, BoatU.S., Mississippi Magazine, Southern Boating,* the *New Orleans Times-Picayune,* and many others. In 2015, he won a Boat Writing International Award for a story on cruising Mississippi's Gulf Islands. Gilbert is also the author of several cookbooks, including *Café Degas Cookbook,* published by Pelican. He lives in New Orleans and is generally either typing on his back porch in Lakeview while sipping wine from his grandparents' old wineglasses or traveling throughout the Gulf Coast, the Caribbean, and Europe writing about boating, culture, and competitive sailing.

Matthew Mayfield claims he first heard the call of the Mississippi State University "cowbell" in his mother's womb while she was cooking shrimp and grits. He was birthed in Pascagoula and eventually attended Mississippi State, where he graduated in 1995. He followed that up with a stint at the Culinary Institute of America in Hyde Park, New York, graduating at the top of his class in 1998. Matthew settled in New Orleans and worked in several fine-dining establishments before moving back to the coast to open his own restaurant in Pascagoula. Today he is co-owner of Tay's BBQ, owned by his wife's family in the 1940s and resurrected in 2002. Matthew lives in downtown Ocean Springs with his wife, Hanna, their twin daughters, and four boats in various states of disrepair.

Raised in the Seacliff neighborhood of Gautier on a bluff overlooking the Mississippi Sound and next door to the Walter Anderson family's ancestral home of Old Fields, Billy Solitario grew up fishing and sailing the Gulf Islands and started sketching and drawing these scenes as a young lad. In 1994, he graduated from the University of South Florida with a B.F.A. and moved to New Orleans. In 1997, Billy received the prestigious Gwendolyn Ozols Scholarship, studied painting full time, and earned an M.F.A. in painting from Tulane University. Today, he is a professional artist and has his own gallery on Magazine Street in New Orleans: Studio Solitario. His work is held in the permanent collection of the Ogden Museum of Southern Art in New Orleans and can also be found at LeMieux Galleries in New Orleans; the Red Bird Gallery in Seaside, Florida; Brown's Fine Art in Jackson; and Pink Rooster Gallery in Ocean Springs. Billy resides in Uptown New Orleans with his wife, Nici, and their son, and he frequently returns to the Mississippi Coast to visit friends and family as well as to fish and work on new paintings.